THE ULTIMATE
CHICAGO CUBS
BASEBALL
CHALLENGE

David Nemec

and

Scott Flatow

TAYLOR TRADE PUBLISHING

Lanham • *New York* • *Boulder* • *Toronto* • *Plymouth, UK*

The authors would like to thank Al Blumkin and Dave Zeman for their help in fact-checking this book.

Copyright © 2007 by David Nemec and Scott Flatow
First Taylor Trade Publishing edition 2007

This Taylor Trade Publishing paperback edition of *The Ultimate Chicago Cubs Baseball Challenge* is an original publication. It is published by arrangement with the author.

Published by Taylor Trade Publishing
An imprint of The Rowman & Littlefield Publishing Group, Inc.
4501 Forbes Boulevard, Suite 200, Lanham, Maryland 20706

Distributed by NATIONAL BOOK NETWORK

Library of Congress Cataloging-in-Publication Data

Nemec, David.
    The ultimate Chicago Cubs baseball challenge / David Nemec and
Scott Flatow. — 1st ed.
        p. cm.
    ISBN 1-58979-327-7 (pbk. : alk. paper)
        1. Chicago Cubs (Baseball team)—Miscellanea. I. Flatow, Scott, 1966-
II. Title.
GV875.C6N46 2007
796.357'640977311—dc22

∞ ™ The paper used in this publication meets the minimum require-
ments of American National Standard for Information Sciences—
Permanence of Paper for Printed Library Materials, ANSI/NISO
Z39.48-1992.

Manufactured in the United States of America.

CONTENTS

| Introduction | | ix |
| Foreword, *Alan Blumkin* | | xiii |

GAME 1

Inning 1	Red-Hot Rookies	3
Inning 2	Home Run Kings	5
Inning 3	Master Moundsmen	7
Inning 4	Peerless Pilots	9
Inning 5	RBI Rulers	11
Inning 6	What Was Their Real Handle?	13
Inning 7	Team Teasers	14
Inning 8	All in the Family	16
Inning 9	Fall Classics	19

GAME 2

Inning 1	Famous Feats	25
Inning 2	Heroes and Goats	27
Inning 3	Cy Young Sizzlers	29
Inning 4	Brazen Base Thieves	31
Inning 5	Stellar Stickwielders	33
Inning 6	Who'd They Come Up With?	35
Inning 7	Memorable Monikers	36
Inning 8	Forgotten Unforgettables	37
Inning 9	RBI Rulers	40

GAME 3

| Inning 1 | Bullpen Blazers | 45 |
| Inning 2 | Home Run Kings | 47 |

Inning 3	MVP Marvels	49
Inning 4	No-hit Nuggets	51
Inning 5	What Was Their Real Handle?	53
Inning 6	Circling the Globe	54
Inning 7	Stellar Stickwielders	56
Inning 8	RBI Rulers	58
Inning 9	Red-Hot Rookies	60

GAME 4

Inning 1	Heroes and Goats	65
Inning 2	Famous Feats	67
Inning 3	Home Run Kings	69
Inning 4	What Was Their Real Handle?	71
Inning 5	Master Moundsmen	72
Inning 6	Moments to Remember	74
Inning 7	Peerless Pilots	76
Inning 8	Red-Hot Rookies	78
Inning 9	Fall Classics	80

GAME 5

Inning 1	Cy Young Sizzlers	85
Inning 2	All in the Family	87
Inning 3	Brazen Base Thieves	90
Inning 4	Gold Glove Goliaths	92
Inning 5	Home Run Kings	94
Inning 6	Master Moundsmen	96
Inning 7	Bullpen Blazers	98
Inning 8	Who'd They Come Up With?	101
Inning 9	RBI Rulers	102

GAME 6

Inning 1	Home Run Kings	107
Inning 2	MVP Marvels	109
Inning 3	Peerless Pilots	111

Inning 4   Gold Glove Goliaths   113
Inning 5   Stellar Stickwielders   115
Inning 6   Shell-shocked Slingers   117
Inning 7   Master Moundsmen   120
Inning 8   Odd Combination Record Holders   122
Inning 9   Red-Hot Rookies   125

GAME 7

Inning 1   Strikeout Kings   129
Inning 2   Who'd They Come Up With?   131
Inning 3   Stellar Stickwielders   132
Inning 4   Team Teasers   134
Inning 5   Tumultuous Trades   136
Inning 6   Jack of All Trades   139
Inning 7   Memorable Monikers   141
Inning 8   Home Run Kings   142
Inning 9   Fall Classics   144

Answer Section   147
About the Authors   169

INTRODUCTION

How dare we call this the ultimate Chicago Cubs baseball challenge?

First and foremost, it's designed to give you, our dear reader, the four things you most want in a baseball quiz book: (1) pleasure; (2) a worthy challenge; (3) an opportunity to learn something new about the game you love and the team, chances are, that many of you find at once endearing and eternally frustrating; and (4) the assurance that you're in the company of quiz masters who know their stuff. In short, you not only want to match wits, you also like to come away from a book like this with the feeling that you've been enlightened in the bargain.

You will be, you have our guarantee, by the time you finish here. What we've assembled is a seven-game World Series of entertainment, innings one through nine, starting off with rookies and ending with famous Fall Classic events, heroes and villains. There's a logic to our structure, of course, as there is to all the categories we've chosen. In fact, we'll alert you right off the bat, as it were, that to score well against our curves, drops and heat you need to be moderately savvy in every on-the-field phase of the Cubs rich history from the inception of the National League to the present day.

That isn't to say, though, that you've got to have a raft of statistics and a host of obscure players at your fingertips. Actually, top marks are there for the taking by anyone who has a reasonable amount of knowledge of the game in general coupled with a good eye for using our clues to zero in on the right answer to even our seemingly most impossible questions.

Before ushering you behind the curtain and showing you how our minds work, first let us show you an example of the type of question we abhor: What Kansas City Royals batter hit into the first triple play in Seattle Mariners history and what Mariner recorded the last out in the play? Unless you happened to see that particular play (which is highly unlikely) or else have a PhD in triple plays (also unlikely), all you can do is throw up your hands and take a couple of wild guesses as to who the two players are. And how much fun is there in that? However, if the question had also provided the clues that the unlucky Royals batter now resides in the Hall of Fame and the Mariner who recorded the last out in the triple play spent most of his career as a backup catcher in the mid-1970s with the Astros, then all the burners would be fired and the question would be a fair one to ask, albeit still not one to our taste.

In a nutshell, that's our approach. A good question doesn't just toss up a mildly interesting but essentially arcane feat. It gives you a reasonable opportunity to nail the player or players who were involved in it by providing enough information about them to allow you to make at least an educated guess. Hall of Famer? Could be Harmon Killebrew who finished his career in KC. But wait! Was Killebrew still around when the Mariners came into existence? No. Then who was? We won't spoil the fun by giving away the answer any more than we'll spill on the 'stros backup catcher, but now you get the idea how we work.

Here we are cobbling away in our workshop on three different levels of questions that are more to our taste:

SIMPLE: Who held the Cubs season home run record prior to Sammy Sosa? Single.

INTERMEDIATE: The Cubs haven't always been known as the Cubs. Their original nickname was the White Stockings and they later were known as Anson's Colts or just the Colts. What was their nickname after Anson left the team prior to their becoming the Cubs? You'll be alone in life forever if you miss the name that sired our present Bruins. RBI double.

EXPERT: The 1953 season was the last in which ML players were permitted to leave their gloves on the field when they came in to bat. Who is the lone member of the 1953 Cubs to play both in a season when players could still leave their gloves on the field and for a pennant winner in a 10-team major league? Being told that Ernie was his teammate in 1953 and later batted against him in the LA Coliseum, Crosley Field and Shibe Park trims this to a two-run homer.

Question 1 is so easy that it merits no clues and rates only a single.

In question 2 you're given fair warning that it contains clues when it's read carefully. Good for you if you've already spotted that our clues sometimes come in the form of word-play, puns or even anagrams.

The clues in question 3 are straightforward and the reward one of the highest offered in our book. In addition, you get a sampling of the standard abbreviations we use throughout the book. Here they're ML, short for major league, and LA, short for Los Angeles. Elsewhere you'll encounter other standard abbreviations such as NL for National League, AL for American League, PCL for Pacific Coast League, KC for Kansas City, ABs for at bats, BA for batting average, SA for slugging average, ERA for earned run average, CG for complete games and OPS for on-base percentage plus slugging average.

We won't spoil your fun by giving away the answers to our sample questions. Consider them a bonus. And, incidentally, there are a number of other bonuses in our book, not the least of which is our invitation to compile your own

BA, SA, RBI and total base totals as you cruise along. There are over 660 at bats in *The Ultimate Chicago Cubs Baseball Challenge* or about the same number you'd get in a season if you were in there for all 162 games. Don't expect to hit above .300, though, unless you really know your Cubs. But by the same token, you have our assurance that not even diehard Bruins fans are likely to outhit readers that have a firm knowledge of all of major league history. This, after all, is the ultimate Cubs test for the ultimate well-rounded fan.

One final note. The statistics in our books in rare cases will differ from those in other reference works and even in a few instances from those accepted by Major League Baseball. An example is Roger Maris's RBI total in 1961. Most reference works continue to credit Maris with 142 RBI and the undisputed American League leadership. However, reliable research has documented that Maris had only 141 RBI in 1961, tying him with Jim Gentile for the AL RBI crown. There are other such occasions when we might present data that is slightly ahead of the curve. But there are no occasions in this book when the correct answer to a question rides on conflicting data.

Now enjoy.

FOREWORD

I am honored to write the foreword for this groundbreaking series of baseball quiz books by Scott Flatow and David Nemec. I first encountered Scott at the Society for American Baseball Research (SABR) New York City regional meeting in 1985. He wrote an especially challenging and compelling baseball quiz for the event, which I consider myself very fortunate to have won. We became close friends soon after that meeting. Scott quickly went on to bigger and better things as both a baseball trivia player and an author. In recent years he has won three SABR National Trivia championships (two team and one individual). Scott's 1995 team set the current SABR team record for the widest margin of victory, and he later posted the highest individual score to date when he won the individual competition in 2001. During that span he also co-authored *The Macmillan Baseball Quiz Book* and penned *The McFarland Baseball Quiz Book*. In addition, he has written numerous quizzes for independent publications.

In 1991, Scott received a call from Steve Nadel, the New York City SABR chapter chairman and host of that year's National convention in New York City, informing him that David Nemec was planning to attend a SABR convention for the first time. Scott immediately contacted me and we both became very excited because David is recognized to be the father of baseball trivia. He had written two books in the late 1970s, *The Absolutely Most Challenging Baseball Quiz Book, Ever* and *The Even More Challenging Baseball Quiz Book*, that are now regarded as the pioneering works in the field. Scott and I first met David in June of 1991 at the SABR New York City National convention for which Scott orchestrated the trivia competition. As a first-time player, David helped his team to narrowly defeat my team in the finals, and an instant bond developed between us.

In addition to *The Absolutely Most Challenging Baseball Quiz Book, Ever* and *The Even More Challenging Baseball Quiz Book*, David is the author of more than 25 baseball books including two quiz books in the 1990s, the indispensable *The Great Encyclopedia of Nineteenth Century Major League Baseball* and *The Beer and Whisky League*, which ranks as the seminal work on the American Association in the years that it was a major league. David is also the co-holder with me of a record seven SABR National Trivia Championships. He has won six team competitions as well as the first individual championship in 1995.

The matchless qualities in David Nemec's and Scott Flatow's new series of team quiz books are their wry wit, their amazing scope and, above all, the fact that they not only test a reader's recall, they also force him or her to think out of the box and in so doing to expand his or her knowledge of our national game. You will never find such tired posers as "Who pitched the only perfect game in the World Series?" or "What year did the Dodgers move to Los Angeles?" Instead you will be constantly challenged to test the depth and breadth of your baseball knowledge from the first major league baseball game in 1871 to the present day. Furthermore, in this unique series of quiz books you are certain to learn a wealth of new information about players ranging from the well known like Babe Ruth and Hank Aaron to such inimitably ephemeral performers as Eddie Gaedel and Shooty Babbit.

In short, Nemec and Flatow inform as well as entertain. Most other quiz books are content to lob questions at you without helping to guide you toward the answer. You either know who hit such and such, or you don't. Your only recourse if you don't is to consult the answer section, shrug and move on. Nemec and Flatow take a very different approach. First they toss a tantalizing and oftentimes completely original teaser to set your synapses firing. Then they crank your brain up to full boil with descriptive clues that are deftly designed to steer the savvy mind toward the answer. And fair warning: the answer is all too often a name that will make you whack your forehead and go, "Wow, how did I ever miss that?" Have fun with these books. I never had so much fun in all my long years as a trivia aficionado.

Alan Blumkin is the only man to win two consecutive individual SABR National trivia championships. In addition, he has made numerous historical presentations at both local and National SABR conventions. He lives in Brooklyn, New York, and is currently resting on his laurels while serving as the chief administrator and question contributor for the annual SABR National championships.

GAME 1

INNING 1
RED-HOT ROOKIES

1 As a Cubs rook, this post-expansion third sacker hit a nifty .313 but would hit for an even better average in each of his next two seasons before being dealt. During his three-year Bruins stay, he belted a blistering .336 across 400 games. Single.

2 It's safe now to say that no one will ever break this Windy City righty's all-time rookie record for wins with 43. Name him for a RBI double.

3 More often seen in a White Sox uniform during his long ML career, he set the current Cubs rookie record for walks when he coaxed 92 free passes in 1943, his lone full season as a Bruin. Double.

4 Chicago plucked this wanna-be shortstop from Detroit of the Western League, converted him to a third baseman and watched him set an all-time record for the highest batting average by a NL rookie with as many as 400 at bats when he lashed a towering .358 for the 1895 crew. Triple.

5 What Cubs rook challenged the NL frosh BA record in 1922 when he slammed .352 in 466 at bats? We'll tell you that he'd previously had a cup of coffee with both Brooklyn and the Red Sox and lasted only four seasons with the Cubs, but if we also told you his nickname, we'd have to award a lot less than a RBI double.

6 Cancer claimed the life of this hurler less than six years after he launched his big league career by posting 20 wins for a Cubs flag winner and topping the NL with an .833 winning percentage. Three bases if you know this regal rookie.

7 A certain pair of Cubs outfielders finished 1-2 in the Rookie-of-the-Year balloting, with one riding a 30-game hitting streak for top honors and the other stroking a neat .324. Wrigley faithful hoped the duo would provide years of thrills, but it wasn't to be. Double for both, zero for less. Add a RBI for the year.

8 His 25 wins in 1888 were once believed to be the Chicago NL franchise's all-time rookie record for a lefty. It has since been established that he threw right-handed, but we'll still throw you a solo homer if you can name this frosh Chitown sensation from nearby Milwaukee who exited the majors two years later with just 32 career wins.

9 Picked seventh overall in the 1974 free-agent draft, this Cub later slapped .289 in 346 at bats as a rookie. Somehow, he played over 400 games in six seasons as a Bruin despite hitting just four homers with a .634 OPS, horrific stats for an outfielder. You're good for two, plus a RBI for the sterling rookie year of this man whose given first name was Vernon.

10 Although he possessed one of the finest curveballs ever, this former Negro leaguer had trouble controlling his repertoire as he walked a post-1900 NL record 185 batters in his frosh year with the Cubs. Take a RBI single, plus an extra base for his yearling year.

AB: 10
Hits: 10
Total Bases: 23
RBI: 6

INNING 2
HOME RUN KINGS

1 In the Cubs last flag season to date, who led them in homers with just 13? Two-bagger.

2 When a certain gardener hammered six dingers in his role as Chicago's top-of-the-order hitter in 1889, he set a record for the most homers leading off a game that was later tied but remained unbroken until 1973. Who was this slugging leadoff man? Tough three-bagger.

3 Who topped the Cubs with 18 homers in 1975 despite missing over 40 games? Subsequently, this stocky Tuskegee, Alabama, slugger punched over 200 homers with a certain AL club and would no doubt have set that team's career mark had he stayed healthy. Double, plus a RBI for his AL club.

4 When Hack Wilson slugged 30 dingers in 1927, whose record for the most homers by a Chicago NL outfielder did he break? Naming him will earn you one of your own into the deepest reaches of the Wrigley bleachers with two aboard.

5 Time for us to groove another one and ask for the name of the Cub who became the first senior circuit swinger to bop three homers on Opening Day. Single.

6 What Cubs first sacker and owner of a lackluster .240 batting average slugged 18 homers in 1914 but lost the NL four-bagger crown when Gavy Cravath of the Phils clubbed 19? RBI triple for the man who hit more career homers off Christy Mathewson than any other batter.

7 The Cubs set a post-Deadball Era record they'd rather forget when 149 Bruins were nailed trying to steal in 1924. Only three Chicago regulars that season were successful in more than half of their theft attempts. Two of them were outfielders Jigger Statz and Cliff Heathcote and the third—and the most successful of all with 10 swipes in 12 attempts—was what future Hall of Famer who also led the club that year in homers with 16? RBI single.

8 After Ernie Banks moved to first base, it would be many years before the Cubs had another shortstop pop as many as 20 homers in a season. Never confused with Ernie, he hit .228 with 59 RBI in 152 games in his 20-dinger year before departing in midseason the following campaign. Single.

9 What Cub tied Hank Greenberg's ML record of 11 multi-homer games in one season? The previous NL high of 10 had been set by a slugger who clubbed over 20 homers in each of his two years in Cubs garb. A single for the new NL record holder and an extra base for the former record holder. No credit for just the former record holder.

10 In 1958 when Ernie Banks was chosen MVP with a NL-leading 47 homers, the Cubs had four other players with as many as 20 homers. The quartet consisted of the team's first baseman and its entire starting outfield. Name all four for a four-bagger. One base for each.

    AB: 10
    Hits: 10
    Total Bases: 23
    RBI: 4

INNING 3
MASTER MOUNDSMEN

1 Who was the only Bruin since 1900 to spin 300 innings in four straight seasons? We'll add that he won over 200 games on his way to Cooperstown and still ante a double that you guess wrong.

2 After eight indifferent seasons as a starter, a certain Cubs righty went almost exclusively to the bullpen in 1958 and lasted 10 more years in the bigs. The AL saves leader with Cleveland in 1960, he had a .596 winning percentage in relief but was a dismal .350 as a starter. RBI double.

3 What Cubs hurler was the last moundsman to date to record four decisions in the same World Series? Single for him, plus a RBI for the year.

4 Keeping in mind that we consider the National Association to have been a major league, can you name the first 20-game winner in history to wear a Chicago uniform? Home run.

5 Who is the only moundsman in Cubs history to rap as many as 100 hits and surrender as many as 100 runs in the same season? That we refer to him as a moundsman rather than a boxman is your first clue; the only other hint you should need to triple here is that he both collected as many as 100 hits and allowed as many as 100 runs on five occasions but only once did he achieve these two feats in the same season. RBI added if you also know the season.

6 Name the Chicago hurler who held the NL record prior to 1951 for the highest winning percentage (.875) by a 20-game winner. Triple and a RBI for his record year.

7 Who was the only hurler to win as many as 100 games in Cubs livery but nevertheless post a losing career record as a Bruin? For ten years this righty slogged through mediocre Cubs teams that never finished above .500, but he won in double figures seven times including a high of 17. Take your time here and score a double.

8 What 20-game winner recorded the lowest season ERA by a Cubs qualifier since World War II? The year before, this lefty actually posted an ERA nearly three runs higher. Double for him and a RBI for his standout season.

9 For those who like number patterns, this master mounds-man is for you. During his Cubs career he had seasonal win totals of 13, 14, 15, 16, 17, 18, 19—and then snapped the chain by leaping all the way to 26. Twice a 20-game winner with Los Angeles in the PCL, he bagged over 300 victories in the majors and minors combined. Double.

10 What Bruin posted the lowest opponents batting average in NL history as a sophomore after leading the NL in this same department as a freshman? Those who know their history will remember that this master moundsman died the same day as Ty Cobb. Double.

AB: 10
Hits: 10
Total Bases: 23
RBI: 6

INNING 4
PEERLESS PILOTS

1 What Cubs team was the first ML club since Boston NL in 1883 to win a pennant after changing pilots in midstream? One for the year and an extra base for the two pilots involved.

2 Who replaced Cap Anson as the Windy City pilot in 1898? Telling you he was an ex-teammate of Cap's shortens this to a RBI single.

3 What Hall of Fame skipper assembled most of the pieces for the Cubs 1906–1910 dynasty? Don't gamble here, it may not be your knee-jerk answer. Double.

4 How many years did Cap Anson serve as the playing manager of the Chicago NL team? Three bases.

5 The name of the manager of the 1918 Cubs flag winner is not on the tip of everyone's tongue, so we're giving a triple here.

6 Plucked from the Cubs broadcast booth, this former AL MVP helmed the Bruins just prior to Phil Wrigley's failed "College of Coaches" experiment. Just a single.

7 Speaking of Wrigley's managerial machinations, name the four men who rotated into and out of the Cubs skipper seat in 1961. Take a single for nailing just one, and an extra base for each of the others.

8 What skipper who guided the Cubs for the better part of three years in the 1970s has the highest all-time career winning percentage (.537) among men who managed as many as 1,000 games but never finished first? A former backup catcher, he steered San Francisco to four straight second place finishes before landing in Wrigley. Departing late in his third season with the Cubs, this aging warhorse was actually collecting Social Security at the time. Double.

9 A .279 stick across 15 seasons, he played regularly for two flag winners during the 1950s. Later, he replaced as Cubs skipper the manager under whom he once starred. Take a single for this southerner, plus a RBI for the helmsman he displaced.

10 He managed the Cubs for five full seasons and once led them to 90 victories. Interestingly, he's the last to date of four Windy City pilots to win that many without ever playing in the bigs. Squirm his name from your memory bank for a single, plus an extra base for each of the other three pilots to make the same claim.

AB: 10
Hits: 10
Total Bases: 23
RBI: 2

INNING 5
RBI RULERS

1 Who led the last Cubs flag winner to date in RBI with 110? Double.

2 Who is the only other Cubs shortstop besides Ernie Banks with a 100 RBI season? RBI single.

3 In 1970, Billy Williams set the team record for RBI in a season by a lefty swinger with 129. Whose former lefty club high did he edge by one?

4 Who was the first Cub to pace the NL in RBI in the 20th century? His total was a mere 83, and your reward is a generous RBI triple.

5 Hack Wilson is now credited with 191 RBI in 1930. What Cub finished third to him in the NL ribby race that year with 134 despite hitting just 13 home runs? RBI single.

6 Hank Sauer led the Cubs in RBI during five of his first six seasons in Chicago. Who kept Sauer from leading the Cubs six straight years? This one's trickier than it looks. Double and a RBI for the year.

7 How many times did Ryne Sandberg lead or share the Cubs team lead in RBI? Single.

8 Who holds the Cubs record for RBI by a first sacker since 1900? True, Jim Hickman drove in 115 in 1970, but he played just 74 games at first. The man you seek anchored the sack for 158 contests and didn't even pinch-hit. Single.

9 In hitter-happy 1894, two Chicago NL slammers, Walt Wilmot and Bill Dahlen, collected 100 RBI, but it would be

17 years before another Cub topped 100 RBI. Who broke the dry spell and led the NL in RBI to boot in 1911? RBI single.

10 Who posted the most RBI in a season by a Cubs player-manager since the days of Anson? In his last year as a regular, he pushed 90 across in only 100 games. Two for him and a RBI for the year.

AB: 10
Hits: 10
Total Bases: 16
RBI: 6

INNING 6
WHAT WAS THEIR REAL HANDLE?

All these Cubs stars are listed in the record books by their nicknames or middle names. Do you know their true first names?

1 Keith Moreland. Triple.

2 Bruce Sutter. Single.

3 Three Finger Brown. Single.

4 Nixey Callahan, with the caveat that fans in his day never referred to him as Nixey but rather by a derivation of his real first name.

5 Dutch Leonard (the Dutch that was so effective in the Cubs bullpen in the late 1940s). Triple.

6 Jigger Statz. RBI three-bagger.

7 Hippo Vaughn. RBI double.

8 Woody English. Home run.

9 Ray Burris. RBI double.

10 Andre Rodgers. Ringing triple.

11 Jim Marshall. Homer.

12 Rip Russell. Three-run shot.

    AB: 12
    Hits: 12
    Total Bases: 33
    RBI: 8

INNING 7
TEAM TEASERS

1 What Chicago NL team set the current all-time senior loop record for the highest winning percentage in a season? Two-run double.

2 When the Cubs won the 1984 Eastern Division flag they sported six players with as many as 80 RBI, but none of them reached 100. A triple for all six, double for four, zilch for anything less.

3 No Chicago NL team has ever plummeted to last place after winning the pennant the previous year. What club came the closest, dropping to next to last? Three-bagger.

4 The first Cubs team to finish in the NL cellar lost only 86 games and wound up a mere two and a half games behind the 5th place Boston Braves. What year are we talking about? Pinch double.

5 What Cubs team set the current post-1900 record for the highest winning percentage in a season by a second-place club? Double.

6 What Cubs crew set an all-time record for the most games lost in a season by a pennant winner to another team in its loop when it was bounced 16 times by the Cardinals? RBI double.

7 What was the first Cubs team to lose 100 games in a season? Two-run single.

8 The only Cubs team since the Deadball Era that failed to cop a league flag despite featuring two 20-game winners is worth a single. But you can dig for two by naming both members of their mound duo.

9 What Cubs crew won 88 games en route to becoming the first big league team to blow away 1,400 batters? Single.

10 What was the first Cubs team to blast 200 homers? That season they boasted the league leader in this category, and it wasn't Sammy. A single for the year and a RBI for their clout king.

11 The 1936 Cubs featured six players who went to that year's All-Star Game. Four appeared in the starting lineup while the two pitchers worked later in the contest. Triple for all six, double for five, zilch for less than five.

12 What was the last Bruins team to feature a player-manager? A double for the year and an extra base for the skipper.

AB: 12
Hits: 12
Total Bases: 25
RBI: 6

INNING 8
ALL IN THE FAMILY

1 The father showed amazing durability, catching 612 of 624 games in his first four seasons as a Cubbie before knee injuries destroyed his resiliency. Although he was never much with the stick, his son excelled as a thumping receiver blasting over 200 dingers, with 28 coming in 512 at bats across two seasons in Wrigley. Too much here for more than a single for both names.

2 Which of the five Delahanty brothers was the only one to wear Chicago NL livery? He debuted, in fact, with the 1901 Windy City crew and is the only one of the sibling quintet to play on a ML flag winner. His first name scores a single and knowing his pennant team and season rates an extra two-base bonus.

3 Short of pitching in 1884, Chicago's player-manager Cap Anson gave the ball in a game at Detroit on July 15 to the brother of the club's career wins leader at the time. The results were disastrous as the younger sib gave 16 hits, tossed five wild pitches and lost 14-0. Knowing the family name will get you to first base, but you can stretch this to a double if you also know the first names of both these box brothers.

4 This Cub holds the big league record for the most consecutive games with as many as one RBI (18), and his son, who was also a first sacker, was later hit in the face by a line drive in batting practice, resulting in the installation of the protective screens you now see in front of both first and third bases during BP. The last name of this history-making duo rates a double, plus an extra base and a RBI if you also know the first names of both these first sackers.

5 This one's guaranteed to rattle your teeth and surrounding tissue. What chucker who debuted with Chicago in 1888 and was the first player in history to be traded three times in his career had a brother who was once erroneously believe to be the first NL player to homer in his first major league at bat? The elder brother was the sheriff of Allegheny County later in life and all of the younger sib's seven ML wins came with Pittsburgh, where both made their home. Two-run blast for the family name.

6 What Cubs rookie centerfielder in 1948 had a sibling born 11 years before him that pitched for Brooklyn in the 1930s? The clue that the gardener later became a full-time bullpen operative for the Cubbies and led the 1955 staff in both appearances and ERA should help you wrap up the family name for a double, plus a RBI for each sib's first name.

7 A blister forced this Cubs starter's removal with one out in the seventh, but luckily his older brother relieved him and preserved the only sibling combined shutout in big league history. Name both husky hurlers for a double.

8 Gift time. Pops played with eight teams and hit the last six of his 332 career homers as a Cub. Five years later, his lad cracked 16 round-trippers as a freshman with another NL outfit but pounded many more thereafter. Single for both.

9 Who were the first brother teammates to play for the Cubs after 1900? The younger sib, a first baseman, paced the International League with 37 clouts the year before he joined his catching brother with the 1971 Bruins. Neither did anything of note in Chicago, combining for 101 at bats that year and hitting an insipid .149. A triple for their surname and a RBI for each sib's first name.

10 In parts of two seasons in the Windy City outfield, sonny collected 416 at bats and stroked a chilly .207 before moving on. But dad also patrolled Wrigley's pasture and hit .291 for a Cubs division winner. The family name will ticket you to first base.

AB: 10
Hits: 10
Total Bases: 22
RBI: 7

INNING 9
FALL CLASSICS

You'll need to know your pre-1901 postseason history to score well in this section, but it gets easier later for the purists who mistakenly prefer to think the first World Series in baseball history occurred in 1903.

1 Long forgotten is the first interleague postseason game ever played. It occurred on October 6, 1882, at Cincinnati's Bank Street Grounds and resulted in the NL champion Chicago White Stockings being shut out 4-0 on seven hits. Who was the bespectacled Cincinnati hurler that white-washed the Chicagoans that day? An easy bloop double for those who know their history.

2 Here's another corker! The following day, on October 7, 1882, what Chicago hurler retaliated by shutting out Cincinnati 2-0 on just three hits and in so doing claimed the first-ever Chicago interleague postseason victory? RBI single.

3 What was the name of the Chicago ballpark that hosted the first interleague World Series game ever played in the Windy City on October 14, 1885? Homer.

4 The 1885 World Series between the NL champion Chicago nine and the AA champion St. Louis Browns ended in an unsatisfying 3-3 tie. Zap the names of the two Chicago hurlers that shared the entire Series workload. You need both for a solo homer and receive just a sacrifice hit for knowing only one.

5 In Game 4 of the 1885 World Series, played at St. Louis, Chicago found itself short a right fielder and called a local Mound City lad out of the stands to fill in that day. The

18-year-old youth went 0-for-4 and was promptly forgotten by Chicago followers. Today, however, he is well remembered by historians as the only player in history to make his ML debut in a World Series game. Even those with a modest knowledge of the 19th century know him as the lone rookie to win a home run crown in the American Association, thanks to his 19 dingers for Cincinnati when he resurfaced in the bigs in 1889, and also as one of the very few men to claim home run titles in two different major leagues. It'll bother you for a long time if you stumble on what could be a two-run triple.

6 Chicago's last postseason game in the 19th century came on October 23, 1886, and ended with a moment that forever became known as "Curt Welch's $15,000 Slide." In truth, however, Welch probably scored standing up on either a wild pitch or a passed ball to give the St. Louis Browns a 4-3 win in 10 innings that sealed the American Association's lone undisputed World Series win over its National League rival. Who were the Chicago pitcher and catcher that were guilty of the gaffe that allowed Welch to score? Triple for both and zip for knowing only one of the pair.

7 What outfielder was blasted after Game 6 of the 1886 World Series by Chicago manager Cap Anson for misplaying Arlie Latham's fly ball in the 8th inning to help give the St. Louis Browns three runs and tie the game, sending it into extra innings and resulting ultimately in a crushing Series-ending Chicago defeat? The clue that he was a former NL batting champ is so generous that we can give only a single here, but we'll add two bases if you know what team he played for when he won his batting title.

8 In that same memorable contest, Game 6 of the 1886 World Series, if Latham's fly ball had been caught the hero of the game in all likelihood would have been Chicago's cleanup hitter that day, who collected the game's only homer and tallied all three Chicago runs. We'll provide the clue that his fielding contribution in that game consisted of just one assist after he'd made 340 assists during the regular season and still grant you a three-bagger

9 Jiggs Donahue's single in the seventh frame was all that prevented what Cubbie from tossing the first no-hitter in World Series history? Worth a single.

10 Who was the last Cub to date to bat in a World Series game? He forced Roy Hughes at second to give the Tigers the 1945 championship after leading all NL regulars at his position in batting at .302. Double for him and a RBI for his position.

AB: 10
Hits: 10
Total Bases: 26
RBI: 6

GAME 2

INNING 1
FAMOUS FEATS

1 The first Cubbie to hammer three homers in a game on four separate occasions in his career performed all four of these feats at Wrigley Field. Too easy to count for more than a bloop single.

2 What Cubs tosser got off to a perfect 9-0 start one year when his season was brought to an abrupt halt by a summons to military duty? RBI single.

3 The first NLer to switch-hit homers in a game in consecutive seasons stroked his blasts in Cubs garb in 1963 and 1964. A year later he was gone from the majors before the age of 30, with just 17 career homers in 215 games. A triple for this forgotten outfielder.

4 The only pitcher in ML history to emerge a complete-game winner in a contest in which he gave up four home runs to a single batter wore a Chicago NL uniform the day he achieved his memorable feat in a 9-8 win over the Phillies on July 13, 1896. Note that he had the same name as a later-day NL batting title winner. Now nail both the hurler and the four-homer slugger for a dinger of your own. Bunt single if you stumble on one of the pair.

5 Who is the youngest pitcher to date to appear in a game for the Cubs? Just three months past his 18th birthday, this pencil-thin lefty would amass 115 career wins in 14 seasons, including 22 one year in Wrigley. Double.

6 What Cub is the only pitcher to open a season by tossing complete-game one-hitters in each of his first two starts? The most underrated NL pitcher of his era, this Arkansas slinger averaged nearly 20 wins during his five peak seasons in Cubs garb. Double.

7 The first member of the Cubs to crush three taters in a game at Wrigley Field is better known for his loony feats with another NL team. Take a RBI double for the name of this Ruthian imitator.

8 The longest relief stint in big league history in a winning effort came, by George, from a Cub in 1915 when he went 18⅓ innings to beat the Dodgers 4-3 in 19 innings. Neat two-run shot into the centerfield bleachers at Wrigley for his name and, of course, zippo for anything less.

9 This Dominican caught over 200 games for six different clubs while flying under most fans' radar. However, one spring day, his moment in the sun came when he tied the nine-inning record for putouts by a dish man with 20. Thinking about how catchers earn putouts should clue you which Cubs moundsman was dealing that day. Three bases, plus a RBI for the hurler.

10 Acquired from the Astros for Davey Lopes, this lefty reliever was a Cubs bullpen workhorse, appearing in 69 games in 1987 and 63 more the following year. Although he took the hill exactly 700 games with five teams, Cubbie rooters remember him best as the first man to win an official night game at Wrigley Field. Triple.

AB: 10
Hits: 10
Total Bases: 25
RBI: 5

INNING 2
HEROES AND GOATS

1 The Cub who yielded "Big Mac's" record 62nd homer in 1998 will only net you a single. But snag an extra base if you remember the teammate who coughed up Mac's 61st shot to tie him with Roger Maris for the most four-baggers in a season.

2 Who was the only Cub to lose his first eight big league decisions? Although all eight of his losses came as a starter, this stellar lefty bullpenner, who tossed from 1960 through 1976, retired with just 35 starts in 584 games. Double.

3 The Merkle Blunder that helped the Cubs win the 1908 flag was prefaced by a similar incident in Pittsburgh several weeks earlier. What was the name of the rookie Pirates baserunner Johnny Evers unsuccessfully tried to have declared a "goat" out at second base on a force play in circumstances almost identical to the Merkle Blunder? Two-run shot.

4 What catastrophic event in 1871 forced the Chicago team to finish the season on the road, leading to the loss of the 1871 National Association pennant? Line single.

5 Game 3 of the 1918 World Series ended in a 2-1 Chicago loss when what Cubs runner was caught in a rundown between third and home while trying to score from second on a passed ball in the bottom of the ninth? He played second base that day, scored the Cubs only run in the contest back in the 5th inning, and might have been a Series hero rather than one of its goats had his misguided attempt to score the tying run in Game 3 been successful. Solo homer.

6 Who hit the Cubs only homer and tied for the team lead with four RBI in the World Series that brought the Bruins their last World Championship to date? Stand-up double.

7 After sitting out the first game, what backup outfielder played the final three games of the 1938 World Series in center field for the Cubs and knocked home all three Chicago runs in Game 2 and both Chicago runs in Game 3 to finish the Series with a .500 BA and a club-leading five RBI? Name the Cubs unlikely hero that year who bore none of the blame for the Bruins being swept by the Yankees and earn a two-run triple.

8 In a colorful 11-year career this brawling third sacker played for five teams including two world champs. Although a .265 lifetime hitter, he struck just .215 in his only season as a Cub. His Bruin nadir occurred on May 2, 1956, when he became the first NL swinger to fan six times in one game. RBI single.

9 What popular Cubs skipper donned goat horns when he was fired during spring training one year after he gave members of the media his candid assessment of the team's chances that season?

10 When the Mackmen scored a record ten runs during the infamous seventh inning of Game 4 in 1929, what Cub suffered the loss? Often overlooked during this era, he won in the double figures six times with the Cubs, including a 17-11 slate in 1928. Control was a problem as he led the NL in walks twice and averaged over four free passes per nine innings in the Windy City. A RBI double for the righty with these arresting stats.

> **AB:** 10
> **Hits:** 10
> **Total Bases:** 20
> **RBI:** 7

INNING 3
CY YOUNG SIZZLERS

1 Rick Sutcliffe won a Cy Young Award for a season he split between the Cubs and the American League. What other 20-game winner for a Cubs postseason entry might have been able to make the exact same claim had there been a Cy Young Award in his day? Double.

2 What recent Cub went a sparkling 20-6 but earned just two third-place Cy Young votes before plunging to 6-8 the following season? Score a single by conjuring up both his name and the year.

3 What hurler won a retrospective Cy Young Award for topping the NL in wins, saves and innings pitched for a Cubs team that won over 100 games but not a pennant? Single for him and a RBI for the year.

4 His second full season in the majors brought a NL-top 22 wins and five shutouts, plus a trip to his first of two World Series in Cubs livery, all in addition to a retrospective Cy Young Award. Double.

5 He was on a flag winner his first year with the Cubs but was called into the military before the World Series rolled around. In his ninth and final year with the Cubs he was traded to the NL pennant winner midway through that season. His third year with the Cubs was his best as he won a NL-leading 27 games, the loop ERA crown and a retrospective Cy Young Award. Two-bagger if you know the hurler who fits this profile.

6 What Chicago hill great had over 100 wins before he logged his first career shutout in 1897 and then proceeded to notch four whitewashings the following year and out-Cy even Cy Young himself when he logged the lowest ERA of any NL qualifier in the 1890s, a glittering 1.88? Double.

7 The best season by far for this 14-year journeyman came in Cubs livery as he went 18-7 and quietly snagged a Cy Young vote when no one was looking the year Mark Davis won it. A single for him and a RBI for the year.

8 In three seasons with the Cubs he won 23 games, two fewer than he totaled during his Cy Young campaign in the AL. Shoulder woes limited him to just four more victories before he returned to Wrigley in another capacity. Single.

9 What Cub captured the Cy Young Award and completed a whopping 30 of 39 starts, the most for a Cubbie since Pete Alexander in 1920? RBI single.

10 Which of these Cubs mound stars never earned a single Cy Young vote while wearing Bruins livery? Ken Holtzman, Lee Smith, Mitch Williams or Randy Myers? Single.

AB: 10
Hits: 10
Total Bases: 14
RBI: 3

INNING 4
BRAZEN BASE THIEVES

1 Who is the only man born in the 20th century on the Cubs all-time top 10 list of base thieves? RBI single.

2 Stolen bases did not permanently become an official statistic until 1886. Chicagoans then had to wait 11 years for their first theft leader. For a RBI double, who was it?

3 Who was the first player in the 20th century to lead the Cubs in steals three straight seasons? A middle infielder, he sparked the Bruins on the base paths with 26, 27 and 26 steals, respectively. Tough triple.

4 He stole as many as 20 bases just once in his long career with the Cubs but won two NL stolen base crowns, each time with less than 20 thefts. Carve out his name for a two-bagger.

5 This Hall of Fame outfielder spent just two seasons with the Cubs but led them in steals both years despite missing over 50 games in the latter campaign. True, his totals were just 16 and 7, but he paced the NL in thefts as a rookie with another outfit and snagged over 200 before he was done, which was the third highest total of any player active during the years his career spanned. Double.

6 Never a .300 hitter in his 10-year career, this outfielder popped a personal best .288 with the Cubs in 1995. A year later he made papa proud by topping the Cubs with 37 steals, the most by a Bruin in over a decade. Single.

7 For years the Cubs lacked a dominant base stealer; consequently only one player pilfered as many as 20 sacks twice between 1938 and 1966. Unfortunately, the Bruins rushed to unload him at age 24 rather than allow him to provide steady work at second for many more seasons to come. Double.

8 Obtained with Fergie Jenkins, this outfielder either led or tied for the Cubs lead in steals during each of his first three seasons, including 32 in 1966, the club high since 1930. Durocher likened him to the "Say Hey Kid," but hindsight left Cubs fans muttering "Say what?" RBI double.

9 Ken Hubbs placed second on the 1963 Cubs with eight steals. However, he would have needed more than three times that many to outstrip the 1963 season's team leader who wasn't long for Wrigley. Name him for a sneaky single.

10 Since the close of the Deadball Era, only one Cub swiped as many as 40 bases twice. He also boasts the Cubs post-1900 season high for thievery at his position. A strong arm and good range offset his lack of pop, which was demonstrated by his mere 14 homers in 2,900 at bats with Chicago. Two bases.

> **AB:** 10
> **Hits:** 10
> **Total Bases:** 18
> **RBI:** 3

INNING 5
STELLAR STICKWIELDERS

1 Who is the only shortstop since 1901 to hit .315 or better in Cubs garb on two separate occasions? RBI triple.

2 His fabled minor league career was highlighted by hordes of black ink, including four batting titles. But for his major league career he had only one .300 season in 1942 to show, and a lone sliver of black ink, that in 1944 when he topped the NL with 12 pinch hits. You'll be furious if you fail to connect for a RBI double on this highly ballyhooed Cubs gardener from the early 1940s.

3 Who was the first catcher in Cubs history to log a .300 BA in a season when he had enough plate appearances according to current rules to be a hitting title qualifier? Triple and two RBI if you also know the year.

4 What Cubs star sandwiched a season in the .250s (.254) in between two seasons when he hit in the .350s (.359 and .352)? RBI triple.

5 Who has stroked the most career singles by any Cub since World War II? Better known for his drives that went further, he posted the highest single season OPS of any Bruin between 1931 and 1997. Single.

6 What second sacker joined the Chicago NL entry in 1900 with a career BA of .316 after his first 11 ML seasons and saw his career mark drop a full 10 points to .306 before leaving both Chicago and the majors after the 1901 campaign? Round-tripper.

7 Since 1900, only two Cubs regulars have rapped .300 for five straight seasons. The first one closed his streak with a

.356 showing, and the latter struck just over .330 only once. A triple for both, a cheap single for one.

8 The last Cubs regular (400 ABs) to rap less than .200 hit .194, the lowest average in the majors that campaign. Ironically, two seasons earlier, he had rapped .283, the highest mark for any Bruin at his position in 20 years. Double.

9 In 1911 what Cubs fly chaser led the NL in runs, walks and OBP? We'll also note that he topped the team in steals with 32 and finished his ML career two years later as the last active performer who had played with a Baltimore team in the National League. RBI double.

10 What Cub once held the NL season record for intentional walks with 29? Knowing that this stat wasn't officially kept until 1955 narrows your search engine. But forget Ernie, although he was the record holder until this Panamanian pastureman, who will be a surprise answer to many readers, eclipsed Ernie by one. A double for him and a RBI for the year.

AB: 10
Hits: 10
Total Bases: 25
RBI: 8

WHO'D THEY COME UP WITH?

Though all of these men were important contributors to Cubs history, they began their careers with other teams. Do you know what their first teams were? The name of the team will score a hit and knowing their exact debut year in each case is worth two extra RBI.

1 Derrek Lee. Scratch single.

2 Fred Pfeffer. Two-run two-bagger.

3 Dutch Leonard. Two-run home run.

4 Hank Sauer. Three-bagger.

5 Hack Wilson. Scratch single.

6 Burleigh Grimes. Tough triple.

7 Kevin Tapani. Triple.

8 Jerry Morales. Double.

9 Kevin Foster. Three bases.

10 Charlie Root. Inside the park dinger.

11 Milt Pappas. Single.

12 Rick Sutcliffe. Single.

    AB: 12
    Hits: 12
    Total Bases: 27
    RBI: 24

INNING 7
MEMORABLE MONIKERS

1 Wildfire. Single.

2 Swish. Single.

3 Dim Dom. RBI double.

4 Dandelion. Double.

5 Little Eva. RBI single.

6 Jolly Cholly. Single.

7 Sarge. Single.

8 King Kong. Single.

9 Mr. Cub. Bunt single.

10 Noisy. Homer.

11 The Gerbil. Single.

12 Smiling Stan. Single.

> **AB:** 12
> **Hits**: 12
> **Total Bases**: 17
> **RBI**: 3

INNING 8
FORGOTTEN
UNFORGETTABLES

1 Among the numerous fly hawks plugged into center field in 1969 after Adolfo Phillips's hand injury in spring training, he was employed the most often. No Cubs rooter, even those still wet behind the ears, should ever forget this unforgettable man Durocher and Santo openly berated after he misplayed two fly balls in one inning against the Mets in 1969. Triple.

2 After topping all NL rookies in several hitting departments in 1892, this Chicago gardener drifted back to the minors early in the 1894 campaign and then languished in the bushes for most of the remainder of the 19th century while many lesser outfielders earned second and third chances in the show. It took two consecutive minor league batting crowns in 1899 and 1900 to overcome what some claimed was a rep for chasing the wives of too many teammates and gain our forgotten hero a return ticket to Chicago late in the 1900 campaign. The following spring he jumped to Washington in the fledgling American League, only to disappear permanently despite hitting a career-best .320. Refuse to cry uncle and work out the clues instead until you triple home two runners.

3 No one's ever satisfactorily explained why this lefty who was nicknamed "Tornado" lay forgotten for almost a full decade in the minors before making his initial big league foray with the 1903 Cubs. Though already nearing 30 in his rookie season, he was good for two 20-win campaigns in Chicago before being traded to Cincinnati in 1906, where he notched yet a third 20-win year. Don't loaf here because there's a triple in the offing.

4 Everybody in baseball liked this sweet-swinging lefty outfielder but never enough to play him regularly again in his 11-year career after he injured his shoulder with Cleveland in 1947 while coming off a season in which he topped the AL in triples. Used mainly as a pinch hitter and backup rightfielder thereafter, he really bloomed in 1950 when he whammed .364 in 41 games with the Cubs, but three years later he was gone after a .198 coda with the last AL team based in St. Louis. Tough enough for a two-run homer.

5 Here's your "Forgotten Unforgettables" grand slam. After hitting .296 as a backup outfielder with the 1920 Boston Braves, a certain rookie was transferred to the Cubs the following spring after going hitless in five tries as a pinch hitter. Platooning in left field with Turner Barber, our man outhit Barber .329 to .314 and knocked home 41 runs in just 245 at bats. Nevertheless he was bid sayonara after that season and Barber was retained. We'll tell you that he had the same name as Washington's regular shortstop during most of World War II and still wager that all including our experts have forgotten this gardener who slipped under most fans' radar even in his day.

6 After debuting in organized ball in 1949, this Brooklyn boy waited 11 seasons for his big league shot. No longer a boy at 32, he hit .275 in 102 at bats with the Cubbies. The next year he patrolled center, stroking .255 in 109 games and uncorking a thrilling game-ending grand slammer with two outs in the ninth against the Braves. After a 27-game showing with the expansion Colt .45s, he departed. Rob us for a trip around the bases behind two teammates with this should-not-be-forgotten's name.

7 Despite missing over a month with shoulder trouble, he finished second on the Cubs to Fergie Jenkins in victories in 1982 and was the club's only starter with a better than .500

record (11-10). Coveted enough by the White Sox to bring Steve Trout and Warren Brusstar in trade, this 6' 4" Pennsylvanian was gone from the bigs after just one more start. Three bags for those who remember him.

8 In 1940 this switch-hitting outfielder came out of nowhere for one unforgettable season in which he belted .313 and topped the Cubs in doubles and triples. Packaged that winter with Bobby Mattick in a swap for Cincinnati second sacker Billy Myers, our performer's average fell 80 points with the Reds in 1941, and he played just nine more ML games the following year before slipping to the minors, where he was soon forgotten. Two-run homer.

9 After Hack Wilson's departure, stability in center field became a huge problem in Wrigley for decades. Here's one of the many should-not-be-forgottens who proved to be no solution. In 1954 this Visalia, California, native posted the poorest OPS of any Cubs outfielder in as many as 400 at bats between the close of the Deadball Era and NL expansion in 1962, an appallingly unforgettable .579, before exiting the big top. Two-run homer.

10 This lefty also hailed from the Golden State and teamed with our previous Forgotten Unforgettable man as a memorable frosh in 1954 going 11-7 with a 3.52 ERA before nose-diving into forgotten land thereafter. But his bloodlines were fine as two uncles had earlier made the majors, with one, Marv, going 12-10 for the 1952 White Sox. Grab a three-bagger, plus two RBI for his uncles' family name, which was not the same as his.

> **AB:** 10
> **Hits**: 10
> **Total Bases**: 35
> **RBI**: 16

INNING 9
RBI RULERS

1 Rogers Hornsby and Ryne Sandberg both had 100-RBI seasons as Cubs second basemen and made the Hall of Fame. Who is only Chicago NL second baseman with a 100 RBI season that is not in the Cooperstown pantheon? RBI double.

2 When Gabby Hartnett notched 122 RBI in 1930 to set the present record for a Cubs catcher, what backstopper's former club record did he break? Two-run triple.

3 Until recently the Cubs have lacked consistent power and production at first base ever since the days of Cap Anson. Not until Ernie Banks in 1962 did the Bruins have a first sacker in the 20th century notch a 100-RBI season. What Cubs gateway guardian fell one short of the 100 mark in 1922? Tough three-bagger for many but not our experts.

4 Who was the lone Cubs third sacker prior to NL expansion in 1962 to notch a 100-RBI season? Your clue is that he also had previously posted a 100-RBI season with the Bruins at another position. Two-bagger.

5 In 1971 Fergie Jenkins became the sole Cubs hurler since 1901 to log as many as 20 RBI in a season. Many Bruins chuckers bagged more than 20 ribbies in a season prior to 1901, however. What Windy City righthander really made his hits count in 1891 when he knocked home 24 mates on just 24 bingles and a .245 BA? Long-standing Cubs followers know him best for his unparalleled rookie winning streak the previous season. RBI triple.

6 In 1884, owing to its tiny home park that led to runs a-plenty, the Chicago NL entry had the top four RBI men in the NL, including the first two 100-RBI achievers in NL history. Playing in a new and more traditional home ground the following year, the Chicagoans showcased what most historians consider to be the first legitimate NL 100-RBI man. Who was he? RBI single.

7 Some stats raise eyebrows, and these numbers should send yours soaring. What Cub posted a .437 OBP with 100 RBI just four years after logging the lowest season OBP ever (.300) by a Bruin during a 100-RBI campaign? Lower your brow and poke a single.

8 From 1955 to 1962, Ernie Banks dominated the Cubs lineup, leading in RBI all but once. Name the outfielder that capitalized on Ernie's eye and knee troubles one season to capture the club lead. Double and a RBI for the year.

9 Obtained in late August the previous year, this Illinois native topped the 1917 Cubs with 61 RBI. Because he's so closely linked with his previous team, which reacquired him after the 1917 season, we think we can add that he once won a bat title and still keep you from gaining a triple.

10 After the 1930 team's unmatched offensive outburst, only one other Bruin drove in as many 100 runs in a season during the decade of the 1930s. Cuyler's broken leg opened up a spot for him, and you can fill it with a double, plus a RBI for the year.

AB: 10
Hits: 10
Total Bases: 22
RBI: 7

GAME 3

INNING 1
BULLPEN BLAZERS

1 What blazer currently holds the Cubs career record for strikeouts from the pen? Too much heat here for us to offer more than a single.

2 What 200-game winner led the 1945 Cubs flag team in saves with five? Remarkably, he made only five bullpen appearances all season to go with his 30 starts and 16 wins. Even more remarkably, this ex-Reds hill star never pitched another inning in the majors. Single.

3 Who is the only Cubs hurler to lead or co-lead the NL in saves four years in a row? Chicago trivia buffs will lope to a double but may need to hustle to get an extra base for the four years in question.

4 The 1948 Cubs tied for the NL cellar, but it was no fault of their top bullpenner who led the club in appearances with 54 and games finished with 27 while compiling a stellar 7-2 record and a neat 3.14 ERA. Alas, it was this 30-year-old rookie's one and only full season in the majors and came nine years after he had debuted with the White Sox by hurling four games in relief. Rates a two-run homer.

5 Two years after he led the Cubs with 12 saves, he topped the most recent White Sox entry to lose a World Series in both saves and relief wins. That's all the info you should need to single, but we'll give a RBI if you also know the two seasons involved.

6 En route to a NL-record 116 wins, the 1906 Cubs compiled 125 complete games in 154 starts, which included two tie games. Nail the rookie righthander who led the team in relief appearances with just eight after learning that he logged a brilliant 7-1 record for the Cubs and went on to lead the NL in Ks as a frosh after being dealt in mid-year to the Cardinals for Jack Taylor. Worth a two-run pellet into the centerfield bleachers.

7 Prior to 1963, three hurlers shared the Cubs season record for saves with a mere 13. The trio happened to be arguably the club's top three relievers to that point in time— Three Finger Brown, Don Elston and Turk Lown. What 200-game winner could have given them a strong challenge for supremacy with 40 career saves, second only to Elston prior to expansion? Hardcore Cubs fans won't struggle to single here.

8 Who was the only hurler to toe the rubber wearing Cubs livery in as many as 300 games without ever starting one? Upon departing the Windy City he held the club's season and career saves record so we can't in good conscience offer more than a single.

9 After exiting the AL, this reliever made plenty of noise his first season in Cubs threads, setting a club record for saves and a big league standard for appearances. Both marks have been shattered since by many others, but the Bruins faithful who witnessed his unique underhand delivery will never forget him. Single.

10 Another AL penman that starred upon arrival in Wrigley set a Cubs record, later broken, for saves in a season by a southpaw with 36. But this feral flinger slipped badly the following campaign before moving on. Although he retired after 1997 with 192 saves, his infamous control problems left him with more career walks surrendered than hits—truly unforgiving numbers for a closer. Single.

AB: 10
Hits: 10
Total Bases: 16
RBI: 6

HOME RUN KINGS

1 After tying Pittsburgh's Ralph Kiner for the NL lead with 37 homers in 1952, Hank Sauer slumped to just 19 homers in 1953. Who led the Cubs that year with 28 taters? Two-bagger.

2 In the 1943 wartime season, the Cubs hit just 52 homers owing to the dead ball in use that year. Over half of them belonged to the 1943 NL homer king with 29. Who was he? RBI single.

3 The first Cub to crack as many as 45 homers in a season and bat under .300 also led the majors that year in dingers. Few pounded them farther than this 6' 6" swinger, but his antics with the press and fans kept him from ever being royally embraced. Single for him and a RBI for the year.

4 In 1902 the Cubs hit a post-1900 club record-low six home runs. Two men shared the team lead, each with two. One was Charlie Dexter and the other man also led the team in errors that year with 72. Don't toy around—this rates a triple.

5 Who was the first Cub to win back-to-back NL home run crowns? He earns a single, plus an extra base for his two winning seasons.

6 The first Cub to crack 30 homers and steal 30 bases in the same season is worth one base, plus a RBI for his groundbreaking 30-30 year.

7 Who led the 1932 pennant winners in homers with a meager 13? Swapped for Babe Herman in November of 1932, this gardener returned, albeit briefly, as a 43-year-old war retread for the 1945 NL champs. Double.

8 Sammy Sosa topped Ernie Banks's career club record for homers in 2004. Whose team mark did Banks break? A single, plus an extra base for the year Ernie became top dog.

9 Who is the only Cubs outfielder since 1920 to collect 500 at bats in a season in which he failed to homer? That year he also paced the NL with 116 walks while hitting .291 in 547 ABs. Far better known for his Hall of Fame efforts with his previous NL outfit, he'll net you a single, plus a RBI for the year.

10 The only player to slam a trio of four-baggers three times in one season did it in Cubs garb. You'd laugh if we rated this more than a check-swing single.

> **AB:** 10
> **Hits:** 10
> **Total Bases:** 16
> **RBI:** 4

INNING 3
MVP MARVELS

1 Who is the only Cub to win back-to-back MVP Awards? Infield hit, plus a RBI if you also know the two years he won.

2 Gabby Hartnett won a NL MVP Award, and so did his predecessor as the Cubs regular catcher, albeit with another NL team after leaving the Cubs. Nail Gabby's predecessor and his future MVP team for a RBI single.

3 What Cub won the first MVP prize ever awarded to a senior loop player? Two-bagger.

4 What Cub was selected the NL's MVP in 1929? RBI single.

5 Gabby Hartnett was selected the NL MVP in 1935 in a close vote over Dizzy Dean. Three other Cubs finished among the top 12 in the balloting. Which of the three had been the NL MVP runner-up in 1932? RBI double.

6 Four Cubs finished among the top 10 on the 1945 NL MVP ballot. Name the Cub that won first prize and the two Cubs pitchers that also finished in the top 10 for a two-run double; no credit if you don't know all three.

7 When Johnny Bench bagged his two MVP honors, which Cub placed second both seasons? Single for him and a RBI for his two runner-up years.

8 What Cub bagged a MVP despite posting an OPS nearly 200 points below the NL OPS leader? True, his figure was the highest seen in Wrigley for nearly 60 years, but he would later surpass that mark twice and get nada. Bunt single, plus a RBI for his award-winning season.

9 Who won a MVP in his first season in a Cubs uniform? Already a seasoned vet, he reached his career high in homers that year and never surpassed it in over 20 big league campaigns. Need him and the year for a single.

10 Primarily a setup man in parts of seven seasons with the Cubs, this lefty screwball artist would later capture a MVP as a closer for a world champ. He's a single plus a RBI for the year he won.

11 When the first "modern" BBWAA MVP was awarded in 1931, who received the most votes of any Cubs player? Although he finished fourth in the balloting and was seemingly just reaching his prime, he never again received a single MVP vote. RBI double.

12 Between 1973 and 1983, what Cub placed the highest in the MVP balloting? He came to the Cubs in a trade with an AL club and left in exchange for Bobby Murcer, among others. Two-bagger.

AB: 12
Hits: 12
Total Bases: 17
RBI: 10

INNING 4
NO-HIT NUGGETS

1 Major League Baseball no longer recognizes a game in which a pitcher allows his first hit in extra innings as a no-hitter. What one-of-a-kind ML game did this highly questionable rule change wipe out of the current record books? Just a single.

2 On July 28, 1875, William Hulbert's Chicago National Association team, the ancient ancestors of the present-day Cubs, became the victims of the first no-hit game in big league history. Who threw it? Solo homer.

3 Bob Feller was the first hurler to throw three no-nos in the 20th century. What short-lived 19th century Windy City wonder boy was the first man ever to twirl three hitless gems in his career? RBI single.

4 The Chicago NL entry was never victimized by a no-hitter in the 19th century. What Phillies hurler who later pitched for two Cubs World Championship teams broke the string by no-noing the Cubs—and in their home park, no less—in the second game of a doubleheader on September 18, 1903? Two-run triple.

5 After Cubs flinger Jimmy Lavender no-noed the Giants in 1915, 40 years passed before a Bruin again notched a no-hit win. Who broke the long dry spell on May 12, 1955, with a 4-0 victory over Pittsburgh? Double.

6 He went 28-44 in parts of three seasons with the Cubs, but he'll always be remembered for no-hitting the dreaded Cards just two days after his trade to the Bruins. This nugget's been too often celebrated for us to offer more than a double.

7 When Sandy Koufax tossed his perfecto against the Cubs, what opposing Bruins lefty pitched the best game in his seven-year career yielding just one hit, a seventh-inning bloop double to Lou Johnson? He's also worth a looping two-bagger.

8 After retiring 26 straight batters, what Cubs hurler walked the Padres Larry Stahl on a 3-2 pitch and then routinely notched the final out of an anticlimactic no-hitter? Single for him and an extra base for the future certain-to-be Hall of Fame umpire who denied him a perfecto by deeming that the crucial pitch to Stahl was low.

9 What Cub at age 22 pitched a no-hitter against the Phillies in just his fourth big league start? Adding that he defeated former Cubs bleacher cheerleader Dick Selma limits you to a single.

10 Who tossed the first night game no-hitter for the Cubs just two years after fashioning a hitless complete-game effort against Atlanta in which he failed to fan a single batter? Single.

AB: 10
Hits: 10
Total Bases: 20
RBI: 4

INNING 5
WHAT WAS THEIR REAL HANDLE?

1 Randy Hundley. Double.

2 Sheriff Blake. Two-run homer.

3 Cap Anson. Single.

4 Wildfire Schulte. RBI double.

5 Gabby Hartnett. RBI single.

6 Randy Jackson. Double.

7 Kiki Cuyler. Single.

8 Brock Davis. Three-run homer.

9 Barney Schultz. Two-run blast.

10 Turk Lown. Double.

11 Dom Dallessandro. Homer.

12 Dwight Smith. Call us generous but we think this one's good for three.

   AB: 12
   Hits: 12
   Total Bases: 30
   RBI: 9

INNING 6
CIRCLING THE GLOBE

1 Who holds the Cubs record for homers in a season by a Canadian-born player? Rookie Vince Barton's 13 in 1931 was the club standard until this potbellied New Brunswick veteran smoked 17 in 340 at bats 70 years later. Single.

2 Not until his debut with the Cubs in 1996 did baseball feature a Singapore-born player. In parts of three seasons as a Bruin he totaled just 45 games. Though most Wrigley rooters have forgotten him, you can knock this bird from his nest for three.

3 Anyone remember the switch-hitting first sacker on the Cubs last flag winner to date who was born in Berlin, Germany? Worth a RBI double to all who recall the World War II Deutschlander that debuted with the 1943 Bruins and stroked a pinch single in the 1945 Series.

4 What first generation Polish gardener finished his career as a member of the first Windy City flag winner in 1876? The knowledge that he was the first player in ML history of Polish extraction should help you leg out a two-run three-bagger.

5 What hurler was born in Puerto Rico and died in Mexico far too soon, just nine years after he racked up 18 wins for the 1943 Cubs and led the NL in shutouts? Those that have visited the stadium named for him would scoff if we awarded more than a RBI single.

6 Race to an inside-the-park homer by naming the Canadian-born backstop who finished his eight-year career with the 1921 Cubs. Your clue is that both his first and last names are the same as those of the early-day star that in 1888 broke

Bob Ferguson's record for the most switch hits by anyone wearing a Chicago uniform.

7 Looking for a break from all these high hard ones? Here it is. Canada's first Hall of Fame inductee spent ten seasons in Cubs flannels, and he's an excuse-me-swing single.

8 Feeling stronger? Poke another single for recalling former Bruins first sacker Hee-Seop Choi's country of birth.

9 Once a member of St. John's College cricket team, he grabbed a PCL bat crown with Phoenix in 1958. Later he became the Cubs regular shortstop when Ernie shifted to first. You'll earn a RBI single for this Nassau nugget.

10 His family fled the Nazis and settled in Hartford, Connecticut, when he was just three. He grew up to appear in 589 games, mostly in relief, across 17 seasons. Close this inning with a single by naming the Poland-born righty that the Cubs squandered in a deal for the man in our previous question.

AB: 10
Hits: 10
Total Bases: 18
RBI: 4

INNING 7
STELLAR
STICKWIELDERS

1 Only one Cub since the 1930s has garnered more than one 200-hit season, and he did it three times. No charity here, we're donating just a single.

2 Who was the first Cubs gateway guardian to lead the club in hits for two straight years in the 20th century? We'll spare you some grief by announcing it's not Chance, Grimm or Cavarretta. A .300 hitter in each of his first two full seasons, he never returned to form and failed to last the decade in which he debuted. Double.

3 What Chicago NL infielder once hit .166, the lowest season BA ever by a performer with as many as 400 at bats? If told that remarkably, two years later, he was second in the NL in home runs per at bat ratio, you're favored to nab a solo homer for this captain of the winter-league Boston roller polo team in the early 1890s.

4 What Cubs second sacker who debuted in 1916 with the White Sox had his career year in his final season when he rapped .286 for the 1922 Bruins in 131 games? Grand slam homer.

5 In 1885, Chicago catcher Silver Flint collected 45 RBI despite hitting just .204. Who broke Flint's Cubs club record for the most RBI on a sub-.205 batting average when he banged home 46 runners on a .204 BA more than a century later? RBI double.

6 What Cubs gardener in his second and final big league season ripped .377 in 87 games, including a staggering

15-for-38 as a pinch hitter? Knowing that an AL gardener with the same nickname crashed 59 homers that same season drops this to a double.

7 Who was the first Cub to collect 400 total bases in a season? Careful, it's easy to go wrong here. Tricky double.

8 Save for Gabby Hartnett, who is the only Cubs catcher to post an OPS as high as .900 (minimum 400 at bats)? After hitting .303 that year with a .937 OPS, his numbers went south. Drifting subsequently to seven other clubs, he never managed to keep his head above water before exiting in 2001. Single for him plus a RBI for the year.

9 By far, this 10-year vet's best season came as a Cubs outfielder when he hit .304 with 24 homers including three in one game against the LA Dodgers. Remembered for his outsized, wire-rimmed glasses, he'll bring you a single, plus a RBI for his big year.

10 In 1997 who became the first Cubs pinch swinger to collect 20 hits and 20 RBI in the same season when he logged 20 base knocks and batted .308 while fortifying the Cubs bench with three homers and 22 RBI? His only other season in Wrigley came seven years earlier when he played 84 games as a pinch hitter–leftfielder. Two bags.

AB: 10
Hits: 10
Total Bases: 21
RBI: 8

INNING 8
RBI RULERS

1 What Cubs gardener set the present club record for the fewest RBI by a batting title qualifier (400 at bats) with 20 in 1916 and then nearly topped his own mark the following year when he knocked home only 21 mates? The clue that he was later involved in a one-of-a-kind trade pares this to a double.

2 In 1953 what Cubs fly chaser set a club record for the fewest RBI by a batting title qualifier with a .300 BA when he scored only 25 mates in 520 at bats and posted a .306 BA to boot? Your clue is he vied with Stan Musial for a NL bat crown a year earlier. RBI double.

3 In 1962 Ron Santo set a new club record for the most RBI with a sub-.230 BA when he plated 83 mates on a .227 BA. Whose old mark of 77 did he shatter? Your clue is that a man who finished his 17-year ML career in a Chicago uniform in 1897 set the mark in 1889. Three-bagger.

4 Unlike most teams, the Cubs have not had a hitter since the turn of the 20th century that garnered 100 RBI in a season on fewer than 10 home runs. Who came the closest when he used his six dingers and NL-leading BA to plate 97 mates? RBI single.

5 What rookie earned an encore season in 1932 when he logged 50 RBI and 13 HR in 1931 despite hitting a meek .238 in just 239 at bats? His soph season, alas, was his big league coda when he dipped to .224, but you'll bag a three-run homer if you rise to the correct answer here.

6 In 1950 what Bruins shortstop plated 81 mates despite hitting just .230? Your clues are that his 21 homers that season were the club high at the shortstop position prior to Ernie Banks and that his son, also a shortstop, set a new family dinger record with 24 in 1979. Too much info here to award more than a single for the names of this pair.

7 Upon joining the Cubs as a free agent, he led the majors with 137 RBI, only to see his total plummet to 79 the following season but still top the team. Although he compiled two more 100-RBI seasons in Bruins garb, his best years were with his previous club. Single.

8 The NL record holder for most consecutive 100-RBI seasons is a Cub, and he'll net you an infield hit.

9 Besides Gabby Hartnett, only one other Cubs catcher totaled as many as 90 RBI in a season. At 6' 4", he was one of the tallest regular receivers to enjoy a lengthy career. A two-time All-Star, this redheaded Georgian's numbers plummeted sharply after turning 30. Single.

10 Arriving straight up in a deal for Randy Hundley, this Cub hit an undistinguished eight homers and drove across just 28 runs in 1974. However, on April 17 of that year, he was a RBI Ruler for a day, whacking three dingers and driving home eight mates. Little else happened during his four-year Windy City stay, so he's good for three.

> **AB:** 10
> **Hits**: 10
> **Total Bases**: 19
> **RBI**: 4

INNING 9
RED-HOT ROOKIES

1 Who was the first NL rookie in history to win a Gold Glove? Knowing this ill-fated Cubbie slapped just 310 career hits makes this worth only a bingle.

2 What Chicago NL hurler holds the all-time record for the most career wins by a pitcher who never won another game after his rookie season? Cubs fans who can reach way back will easily smack this one over the ivy; others will struggle.

3 Who led the NL in hits in his frosh season in the course of having the best year in history by a Cubs rookie shortstop? Triple and a RBI for his super rookie season.

4 Some Cubs fans well remember the hurler that logged the most wins by a Cubs rookie since the end of World War II, but most will have trouble nailing this frosh 15-game winner. Double.

5 Who replaced injured second sacker Billy Herman as rookie in 1934 and then played left field for the 1935 NL champs and led the senior loop in runs in his first full major league season? Two-run single.

6 His career record is 4-13, all of it compiled in 1948, his rookie season. It's worth a three-run homer if you know this wild lefty who began and ended his big league stay on a winning note but in between lost a Cubs-record 13 straight games.

7 From 1962 through 1986 the Cubbies failed to produce any pitchers who earned a single Rookie of the Year vote. However, that skein ended when this Texas-born righty went 8-3 as a starter and spot reliever in 1987. In five seasons with Chicago he appeared in 232 games, more than any other Bruin during that period. RBI single.

8 Overshadowed by Darryl Strawberry, this Cubs frosh tagged 17 homers, hit .283 and topped NL rookies with 23 doubles, all while missing 50 games. A year later he went bye-bye in a tumultuous June trade that paid the Cubbies immediate dividends in the form of a division crown. Single.

9 Named the PCL MVP in 1963, he debuted with the Cubs that September and then played 139 games the next year, smacking 19 homers and leading a bumper crop of NL frosh with 12 steals. Somehow he kicked around with six teams until 1972 without ever totaling more than 183 at bats in any other season. Double.

10 Prior to serving as a regular on a NL pennant winner, this first baseman slapped over .290 in each of his three full seasons in Wrigley, including a team-leading .304 as a frosh in 1946. RBI single.

AB: 10
Hits: 10
Total Bases: 20
RBI: 9

GAME 4

INNING 1
HEROES AND GOATS

1 Whose "homer in the gloamin'" was instrumental in bringing the 1938 NL pennant to Chicago? Single.

2 After belting a two-run homer to give the Cubs an early lead in the deciding game of the 1984 NLCS, he went from hero to goat by allowing Tim Flannery's sharp grounder to shoot between his legs and tie the game. Scratch single off his nefarious glove.

3 Few players have posted the top batting average in the majors in both the regular season and the postseason. What Cubs hero can make that claim? Single, plus a RBI for his magic year.

4 Whose looping liner to left field that bounded over Hank Greenberg's head in the bottom of the 12th inning scored pinch-runner Billy Schuster all the way from first base and gave the Cubs their last World Series win to date, 8-7 in Game 6 of the 1945 Fall Classic? Chop your way through the clues to this Chicago "King for a Day" and score a RBI double.

5 Most observers would agree that the Cubs ultimate World Series hero is their career leader in postseason wins. Easy single.

6 Whose loss snapped the Cubs 21-game winning streak in 1935? Although he wore goat horns that day, this lefty won 95 games in Bruins attire and could have finished with over 200 career victories had Uncle Sam not intervened. RBI double.

7 Who is the only Cubs pitcher to win consecutive All-Star Games? Adding that Vida Blue and Steve Carlton were the NL starters in each of those contests makes this a Texas League single.

8 This rightfielder's muff allowed the Red Sox their only two runs in what proved to be the deciding game of the 1918 World Series. Before slamming the horns on him alone, note that the Cubs starter walked the two men who scored and allowed 11 free passes in the Series. Grab a two-run triple for both but just a single for one.

9 Despite his eye-popping .647 postseason average and eight RBI, the Cubs managed only one win in that year's NLCS. Single for the hero, plus a RBI for the year.

10 Coin yourself a triple by naming the wee Scotsman with the heroic name that debuted anything but heroically with the 1881 Chitown flag winner by hitting just .204. When he followed with a .199 season in 1882, it earned his release to the American Association where he scored an amazing 122 runs for Cincinnati in 1887 on just 112 hits.

AB: 10
Hits: 10
Total Bases: 16
RBI: 4

INNING 2
FAMOUS FEATS

1 The first Chicago entry to bag a major league pennant was also the only club to feature a performer that twice made six hits in a game in the same season. His feats came in contests that were only three days apart in July of 1876. Learning that he was a former member of the legendary 1869 Cincinnati Red Stockings shaves this to a RBI single.

2 Since the current pitching distance was set in 1893, on 11 occasions the Cubs have had a hurler register fewer than 100 strikeouts while working 300 or more innings. Chances are you'll be as surprised as we are if you homer by naming the last tosser to date to accomplish this feat in Cubs garb.

3 The first pitcher in big league history to fan as many as 250 batters in four straight seasons did it in Cubs threads. You're up for a slow-rolling single.

4 Who is the only receiver since 1900 to catch two no-hitters thrown by Cubs pitchers? Both games came in the same season that this former iron-man receiver stroked a woeful .218. Take a single for him and a RBI for the year.

5 Who was the lone hurler prior to NL expansion in 1962 that managed to no-hit the Cubbies in the park we now call Wrigley Field? Double.

6 The 1969 season marked the debut of the Cubs "Bleacher Bums" and also the death of the last living man to throw a pitch in a major league game from the 50-foot distance. He graced a major league field just once, on August 13, 1892, while wearing a Chicago NL uniform. Grand slam homer for this one-game hurler who had to leave the contest early that day in order to distribute evening papers to the newsboys on his route.

7 In 1938, who almost single-handedly carried the Cubs to a World Series date with DiMag by leading the NL in wins, shutouts, winning percentage and ERA? Just a single for this native of Plaquemine, La.

8 Although it's been eons since the Cubs have had a super base thief, a Windy City gardener still shares the NL record for the most thefts in a game, thanks to his super performance on June 25, 1881, when he swiped seven bases in Chicago's 12-8 win over Providence. Who is this early-day Chitown star? Triple, plus a RBI.

9 The first man to hit for the cycle in a game in which he also served as a pitcher was a member of Cap Anson's crew on the September day in 1887 when he performed his memorable feat and also earned a win after relieving starter Mark Baldwin. Worth a RBI triple.

10 Ernie Banks is the only man to play 1,000 games at shortstop and over 2,000 games in Cubs livery. Who is the only man to play 1,000 games at first base and over 2,000 games in Cubs threads? Single.

AB: 10
Hits: 10
Total Bases: 21
RBI: 8

1 In 1929 the Cubs for the first time in their history had five home run hitters reach double figures as Hack Wilson raised his own Cubs four-bagger record of 31 (set the year before) to 39. What other Cub also hit 39 in 1929 to share the new club record with Wilson that would last only one year? Single.

2 Who placed second to Sammy Sosa in homers by a Cubbie during the 1998 and 1999 seasons? This Dominican slugger socked 31 and 26, respectively, and then cracked 18 more in 259 at bats in 2000 before changing uniforms that summer. Single.

3 In 1920, while Babe Ruth was hitting 54 homers to set a new ML record, the Cubs were led with a more modest 10. What former NL home run champ topped the Cubs that year in taters? Solo homer.

4 In 1927 Hack Wilson led both the Cubs and the NL with 30 homers. Who was the Cubs runner-up with 14? Our clue that he later set an all-time ML record in another offensive department still makes this a triple.

5 In 1930, when Hack Wilson set the new NL tater record with 56, three other NLers hit more than 30 homers. All, like Wilson, were outfielders, two of the three later won NL home run crowns of their own and two of the three later played for the Cubs. Name all three for a double, no credit for less.

6 Who was the only member of the Cubs to hit as many as 40 home runs in a season between Hack Wilson's record setting year in 1930 and the arrival of Ernie Banks? Single for him, plus an RBI for his 41-homer year.

7 Who was the first Cub to blast 20 homers in a season in which he collected fewer than 300 at bats? This outfielder played for seven teams in 13 seasons, but in two stints as a Cubs part-timer he blasted 59 seat-reachers in 908 at bats. In 1999 he walloped 20 in only 253 Bruin at bats, just six years after sending 10 skyward in 87 ABs for the Wrigley inhabitants. Single.

8 Every savvy Cubs fan knows Gabby Hartnett was the first receiver in ML history to whack as many as 30 homers in a season. But can you name the next Bruins dish man to do so? Single for him, plus a RBI for the year.

9 Who led the Cubs with 23 homers in 1980 while posting a putrid .281 OBP? That was the second and last season he spent in the Bruins pasture, as he hit a pitiful .227 with just 38 walks in 141 games. Double.

10 Who was the first Cubs infielder—first basemen included—to lead the NL in homers after Ernie Banks nabbed his last four-bagger crown? A dribbler up the middle lands you at first.

> **AB:** 10
> **Hits:** 10
> **Total Bases:** 17
> **RBI:** 3

WHAT WAS THEIR REAL HANDLE?

1 Manny Trillo. Triple.

2 Corey Patterson. RBI single.

3 Riggs Stephenson. Solo homer.

4 Peanuts Lowrey. RBI double.

5 Hack Wilson. Single—hey, he's a Hall of Famer!

6 Fred Pfeffer. Two-run homer.

7 Terry Larkin. Three-run homer.

8 Moe Drabowsky. Off-field triple.

9 Tuffy Rhodes. Single.

10 Turk Wendell. RBI triple.

11 Frank Demaree. Just over the fence.

12 Pat Malone. Homer.

AB: 12
Hits: 12
Total Bases: 34
RBI: 11

INNING 5
MASTER MOUNDSMEN

1 What Cubs hurler led the NL in winning percentage three years in a row? Double for him and extra base for the three years.

2 The rules were very different in baseball's early days and walks were few. In 1876, Al Spalding set a Chicago NL record that will almost definitely never be broken when he allowed only 0.44 walks per every nine innings pitched. Since the present pitching rules were established in 1893, who is the only Cubs tosser in enough innings to qualify as an ERA leader to fashion a season in which he allowed less than one walk per every nine innings pitched? Double.

3 What tall Texan's first two full NL seasons with Chicago resulted in a glittering composite 2.61 ERA in 445⅓ innings but only a 19-31 record? After that his luck got worse. By the time he finished his ML career in 1904, he had a 2.72 ERA but only a .374 winning percentage, the poorest of any pitcher in ML history who toiled as many as six full seasons in the majors and posted a career ERA below 3.00. Need we add he died less than four years after hurling his last big league pitch? Our candidate for the best pitcher that almost nobody has ever heard of rates a tape-measure homer.

4 Before Carlos Zambrano did it in 2006, it had been quite a long while since a Cubs chucker paced the NL in winning percentage. A 16-8 slate with a 2.75 ERA placed him fifth in that year's race, and you can score one base for his name and a RBI for the year he first earned Cy Young votes.

5 Seasons come and seasons go. Do you know how many seasons have passed since a Cub last topped the NL in the best strikeouts to walks ratio among ERA qualifiers? We'll clue you that this prudish southpaw also paced the NL in the best opponents' batting average (.228) and best opponents' on-base percentage (.256). Tough RBI double.

6 Who posted the lowest career ERA since World War II among hurlers who worked as many as 1,000 innings in Cubs threads? This one's tougher than it looks, so believe it or not we're dishing out a triple here.

7 Although Ernie Banks made number 14 famous in Chicago, the first Cub ever to don this number won 152 games in Bruins livery, including 20 in 1933. There's no beating around this guy, so we'll award you a gift double.

8 His brief Cubs career consisted of three appearances in 1970. Of course he was already age 47, but he'd hang on elsewhere for two more years before Cooperstown called for him in 1985. Single.

9 Between 1967 and 1973, Fergie Jenkins started on Opening Day every year except one. That season a 23 year-old sophomore got the nod and proceded to notch 14 wins. Dealt early the following campaign, he lasted until age 43 and finished with over 200 victories. Double for him and a RBI for the year he started instead of Fergie.

10 In parts of six seasons, all with the Bruins, he won just 32 games before bowing out at age 28. But in 1938 this righty went 19-12 and yielded just seven homers in 270 innings of work. Two-run double for the Virginian whose given first name was Claiborne and whose son played end for a Big Ten champ at Ohio State.

AB: 10
Hits: 10
Total Bases: 24
RBI: 6

INNING 6
MOMENTS TO REMEMBER

1 Who was the first player chosen number one overall by the Cubs in the June free agent draft? A terror at Thomas Jefferson High, this Brooklyn boy lasted 18 years with a variety of big league outfits while playing over 1,200 games for the Bruins. Single.

2 Believe it not, through the 2006 season just one Cubs pitcher has ever started an All-Star Game. Knowing that he lived until the ripe old age of 94 reveals that it's been awhile. Snag a double for him and a RBI for the year.

3 In parts of five seasons in Cubs gear, he won in double figures twice during the 1990s. But on June 16, 1997, he etched his name into Chicago baseball annals by winning the first regular season game between the Cubs and White Sox. Even modern-day Bruins fans may stumble when digging for a deuce here.

4 The first two Chicago NL players to hit three home runs in a game accomplished this feat not only in the same season but also in front of a home audience. What year were Windy City fans first treated to not one but two such Memorable Moments? Not hard if you know your Chitown baseball history, so this is only a RBI single.

5 What former Giants star slammed three home runs in front of a Wrigley crowd in the first game of a July 4 doubleheader in 1939 not long after he joined the Cubs? Three-bagger.

6 What Cub tied a NL record when he slapped two hits in the ninth inning of the second game of a twin bill in 1927?

For his sake, even after telling you his real first name was Floyd and his first hit in the inning came as a pinch hitter, we'll still award a two-run homer.

7 What Chicago-born righty collected the victory on the day in 1922 that the Bruins and Phillies staged the highest scoring game in NL or AL history, won by the Cubbies 26-23? Triple.

8 What Cubs rookie shortstop gave opposition fans a rare treat when he collected four errors on April 15, 1941, to set all-time records for both the most errors on Opening Day and the most errors by a player in his first major league game? RBI double.

9 Fried by all those big extra base blows coming on questions about Bruins from the dark ages? Here's your chance to score high in the post-expansion era. On September 3, 1970, Leo Durocher rested Billy Williams, thereby ending Williams's NL record 1,117 consecutive games played streak. We're offering a homer if you recall the 29-year-old Mississippian Leo penciled into left field that day.

10 Every serious Cubs fan will romp to a single by naming the Bruins hurler who blanked Brooklyn in both ends of a twin bill in the heat of the 1908 pennant race.

> **AB:** 10
> **Hits:** 10
> **Total Bases:** 24
> **RBI:** 6

INNING 7
PEERLESS PILOTS

1 The lone pilot to date to manage the same team for all or part of four of its pennant-winning seasons and never make the Hall of Fame was also part of the Cubs bizarre manage-by-committee experiment just prior to expansion. Name him for a single.

2 Score a RBI single for the name of the ex-Cubs catcher who sat at the helm when Ernie won his-back-to-back MVP Awards.

3 What umpire who played a key role in the Merkle Blunder served as the Cubs pilot the year Johnny Evers led the Boston Braves to the World Series? Single and an extra base for the year.

4 Who was the first member of the famed Cardinals "Gas House Gang" to serve as a Cubs skipper? RBI double.

5 The name of the man at the helm of the only Cubs pennant winner during Hack Wilson's stay with the team will be easy for older Cubs fans but may elude some of the younger breed. Hence we'll allow a two-bagger, plus a RBI for the year.

6 Who piloted the Cubs at the start of the first season they finished in the cellar? Take a solo homer, plus a RBI for each of his two successors that year.

7 Bruce Sutter's first big league manager poked 11 homers while sharing first base duties with Dale Long for the 1959 Bruins. Score a double for this Danville, Illinois, native.

8 Before piloting the Cubs, this man hopped between second and third for two seasons in Bruins garb. While he experienced success at the helm in the Windy City, others remember him as the linchpin in the deal that cost the Cubs Ron Perranoski. Double.

9 The only skipper to guide the Cubs for an entire season in which they lost as many as 100 games had more success elsewhere. Nonetheless, he finished with a winning record in over 1,000 games at the Cubs helm. He's just a single.

10 A Cubs coach for four years, he managed them for just one game. However, eight years before, while serving as a stopgap skipper, he sat at the helm of an AL world champ. Since his Bruins stint was brief, we'll award a generous double.

   AB: 10
   Hits: 10
   Total Bases: 18
   RBI: 7

INNING 8
RED-HOT ROOKIES

1 Lick your chops and fatten up on the Cooperstown inductee who holds the current Cubs freshman record for homers in a season with 25. Slow-rolling single.

2 Cubs fans salivated early in the 1955 season when this smooth-swinging lefty gardener got off to a hot start and seemed a lock to capture Rookie of the Year honors. He soon cooled down but still finished with 12 home runs on just 57 hits and a meager .218 BA. Further minor league seasoning failed to patch the holes in his stroke, and he had exited the majors by 1959 after hiking his career BA only as high as .223. Pipe up with his name and grab a three-run homer.

3 What second sacker set the Chicago 19th century rookie home run record in 1895 with eight dingers in his first 97 ML games before clashing with manager Cap Anson and being banished to the minors, never to return? Two-run homer.

4 What Cubs hurler had a dazzling 1.54 career ERA after his first three major league seasons, including an awesome 1.42 in his rookie year? He finished with the 1917 Boston Braves and your chances for an expert rating are mighty slim if you don't collect a RBI single here.

5 He won a spot in the Chicago rotation the following year after going 5-0 in five late-season starts in 1898. Later he returned to the club after a stint in St. Louis in time to share the glory the 1906 team achieved with its NL record 116 wins. In the years between 1898 and 1906, at one juncture he set an all-time ML record for tossing the most consecutive complete games. RBI double.

6 After years of trying, Cap Anson finally convinced a certain hurler to give up his cushy railroad job and join Anse's Chicago club. After bagging 16 wins as a rookie in 1889, Anse's acquisition went on to log 166 more career wins, the most prior to 1901 by any hurler past the age of 30. Our clue that he had two 40+ win seasons reduces this to a double.

7 At age 22 he became the first Cubs freshman in over 30 years to lead the team in victories during a non-strike season. Unfortunately, after his sophomore campaign, he endured three operations, including Tommy John surgery, and it took him five years to resurface in the majors. We'll provide you with just a single if you nail this Venezuelan chucker. Single.

8 We can't go more than a single for the Cubs frosh who set a record, later broken, for the highest strikeouts-per-nine-inning ratio in history.

9 Who was the Cubs only free-agent draft pick to date to make his pro debut with the Bruins without having played even a single day in the minors? A University of Texas standout, he went 35-3 with the Longhorns before his unveiling against Steve Carlton. Winner of 151 games, like too many other Cubs hurlers of the era, his best seasons occurred elsewhere. Single.

10 In 1961 what 24-year-old southpaw paced NL rookies with 10 victories on a Cubs team that won just 64 games? Gone from the bigs just two years later, he's remembered by some Bruins rooters as the performer they swapped for Bob Buhl. RBI double.

AB: 10
Hits: 10
Total Bases: 19
RBI: 8

INNING 9
FALL CLASSICS

1 After roaring to 116 wins in the 1906 regular season, the Cubs were expected to easily dispose of their South Side rivals, the White Sox, in the first ever 20th century intracity World Series clash. Instead, the so-called "Hitless Wonders" outhit the vaunted Cubs by three points and claimed the Series in six games. Come within five points of the Cubs team batting average in the 1906 Classic and score a single.

2 A 3-3 twelve-inning tie in Game 1 was all that kept the Cubs from sweeping the Tigers in four games when the 1907 Classic was over. What West Coast product drew the starting assignment for the Cubs in Game 1 and three days later went the route in his 6-1 win over Detroit in Game 4? The clues are there for an opposite-field double.

3 What gardener led the Cubs with four RBI and six stolen bases in the 1907 Series but failed to see action in either the 1906 or 1908 Fall Classic even though he was a Bruins outfield regular all three seasons? Solo homer.

4 Who was the only member of the legendary Tinker-to-Evers-to-Chance infield who did not play in one of the four World Series the club participated in while the quartet was intact? The only clue you should need is that he collected 108 walks but just 114 hits during the regular season the year that ill health kept him out of the Series. Single and a RBI for the Series he missed.

5 Hack Wilson rapped .471 in the 1929 World Series but harmed the Cubs chances when he not only failed to homer but also collected zero RBI. Rogers Hornsby was also little help, notching just one RBI, and an injury held Gabby

Hartnett to just one at bat in the Series. What other Hall of Famer on the 1929 Cubs tied for the club Series lead in both runs (4) and RBI (4)? Double if you slide hard.

6 What Cubs hill stalwart started both Game 4 of the 1929 Series, in which the Cubs saw an 8-0 lead disappear when the A's scored a Series record 10 runs in the last of the 7th inning, and Game 3 of the 1932 Series, in which he lasted just long enough to surrender Babe Ruth's famed "called shot" homer in the top of the fifth inning? Single.

7 In the 1938 Series, what Hall of Famer pinch-hit for Cubs shortstop Billy Jurges in Game 3 and grounded out against the Yanks Monte Pearson and then was fanned by Red Ruffing while batting for Charlie Root in Game 4? RBI double.

8 The only player since 1920 to log at least one .300 season as a regular with each Chicago ML team went 0 for 12 for the Bruins in the 1938 Series. Although gone from the majors a year later, he hit .302 in nearly 4,500 career at bats. RBI double.

9 What Cub is the only pitcher to toss a shutout in three consecutive Fall Classics? Don't expect more than an infield single here.

10 Who started both of the Cubs last two World Series wins to date? If you've pawed awhile at nothing but empty air, we'll take pity by telling you that in his first Series start he surrendered just one hit. Single.

AB: 10
Hits: 10
Total Bases: 17
RBI: 4

GAME 5

CY YOUNG SIZZLERS

1 Cy Young was all of nine years old the year a certain Hall of Fame righthander helped a Chicago NL entry roll to the first pennant in Windy City history and won his 200th career victory and a retrospective Cy Young in the doing. Just a single.

2 From 1963 through 1966, Sandy Koufax was so dominant that only one other NL hurler earned any Cy Young votes. Somewhat surprisingly, he was a Cubbie. Snag a single for him and a RBI for the year.

3 Between 1965 and 1976, only two Cubs garnered Cy Young votes. You know one of them was Fergie, but can you name the veteran righty whose 17-7 slate, coupled with a 2.77 ERA, snatched the other three? Double for him and a RBI for his fine year.

4 Few pitchers can lay claim to deserving a Cy Young Award for a season when they set a club record for losses, but this Chicago fireballer's main competition for the retrospective honor the year he tasted 36 defeats to go with his loop-high 37 wins came from none other than Cy Young himself. Name him for a double and take a ribby for also knowing the year.

5 Had the Cy Young Award been originated the year after Cy retired, what Cubs hurler might have become not only the award's first winner but also its first rookie recipient on the basis of his loop-leading 26 wins and 28 complete games? You need both the year and the hurler to collect a two-run double.

6 What Cubs Cy Young recipient began his award season with a 4-5 slate and an ERA of 5.15 after his first 15 starts? Double.

7 Two years before edging former Bruin Joe Niekro for the Cy Young, he had what was actually his best season when he posted a 1.34 ERA but earned just five votes. He's a single and his winning year is worth a RBI.

8 By adding five victories to his total from the previous year and shaving more than a full run off his ERA, this Cub earned 20 of the 24 first place votes for the Cy Young. You must nail both him and the year for a single.

9 Steve Carlton was the writers' Cy Young pick, but this performer was just as deserving if not more so, notching 20 victories with a Cubs team that earned 20 fewer wins than Carlton's crew. One base for him and another for the year.

10 Besides Fergie, who is the only other Cub to date that was born outside the U.S. to notch a Cy Young vote? A 16-8 slate with a 2.75 ERA placed him fifth in that year's race, and you can score one base for his name and a RBI for the year.

AB: 10
Hits: 10
Total Bases: 14
RBI: 7

INNING 2
ALL IN THE FAMILY

1 Papa caught over 350 games in four years with the Cubbies in the 1970s and hit just .217. But sonny boy was so beloved by Oakland's Billy Beane that *Moneyball* author Michael Lewis called him Beane's "picture bride." Knowing that this promising current swinger clubbed 21 homers as a rook lowers this combo to a single.

2 In 1945 the younger sib in a certain baseball family hit his first ML home run as a member of the Cubs while his elder brother was hammering five dingers with the Reds. Four years later the younger sib hit his last ML homer as a member of the Boston Braves, but his older sib was just getting his batting eye in focus as he clouted 27 home runs for the Cubs in just 96 games in Bruin livery. Name both of this pair for a two-bagger.

3 No question, this one's worth a homer and then some. In the mid-1930s the Cubs tested a certain Coast League slugger as an infielder and found him wanting there but then gave him a whirl again later in the decade after he became a pitcher. Again he came up short of the requisite skills, as did his brother, who was tested at shortstop by the Philadelphia A's in the same time frame. Their real first names were Robert and William, but the Cubbie was known by a nickname that was a derivative of his middle name and is the same as that of Cleveland's sensational rookie 20-game winner in 1948. Four-bagger if you nail all three players profiled here; just a single if you know only the Indian.

4 Here's where the jig is up for self-proclaimed trivia experts who lack overall expertise. Just one season in big league history has witnessed a brother duo that combined to produce both 200 or more runs and 200 or more innings pitched. If this feat had occurred anytime recently, it would have received a megaton of attention. But it didn't and what's more the two sibs that perpetrated this one-of-a-kind achievement not only were given no credit for it at the time it occurred but languish in almost complete obscurity to this day. Only one of the sibs wore Chicago NL garb the year of their dual feat, but the previous season these two Oregon natives had been Windy City teammates before the pitching half was traded to Cincinnati. Three-run shot for the names of this dynamic duo and an extra RBI for the year of their feat.

5 Name the future Hall of Famer on the 1935 Cubs flag team whose son compiled a 3.000 career slugging average as a member of the White Sox. Learning that both were born in Chicago shaves this to a double.

6 Who tallied 94 runs for the Cubs last flag winner to date 22 years after his father stroked a neat .447 in 19 games after coming to the Yankees first World Championship team late in the season from the White Sox? Learning that both father and son were middle infielders born and raised in the Windy City should guide you to a two-bagger if you know both; zero for less.

7 The first son in ML history whose father was also a former major leaguer debuted with the 1903 Cubs on July 2 and was KO'd in the third inning of his only start with the Bruins. His father had earlier been not only a player in the bigs but also a manager and an umpire. The last name of this notable first family rates a RBI single, plus an extra base for both first names.

8 Who were the first brothers to start against each other as ML rookies? The older sib began with the Phillies and traveled to eight other teams in his 15-year career before becoming a pitching coach. Baby bro started with the Cubs, and his best two win seasons combined outdistance the elder's career total. The latter is too renowned to offer more than a single for both brothers.

9 These Alice, Texas, boys were born a year and a half apart and both debuted for the Cubs. The younger sibling began in 1972 and kicked around Wrigley for parts of three seasons before moving to Oakland for his coda. Four years after his brother's unveiling, the elder sib played 30 games before vanishing. Take a four-bagger for nailing the surname and a RBI for each first name.

10 We have a shortstop who played 19 seasons, two of them with the Cubs in the mid-1980s. A fading vet by then, he split time between short and third as a part-timer before returning to the NL West club he debuted with in 1971. His son's big league unveiling came with the Cubs in the form of a one-game relief appearance in 1998. Although that was it for him in the Windy City, he did stick in the bigs and appeared in 72 games for the 2003 Rockies. Single.

AB: 10
Hits: 10
Total Bases: 23
RBI: 8

INNING 3
BRAZEN BASE THIEVES

1 When Stan Hack set the current NL record for the fewest stolen bases by a league leader with just 16 in 1938, what outfielder who turned 35 before spring training started that year was second to him on the Cubs with nine? Triple.

2 The first player in the 20th century to swipe home twice in the same game pulled off his feat in Cubs garb in 1910. Amazingly, despite his two brazen thefts, he tallied only 40 runs that year but two years later racked up 80 runs in his 11th and last full season as a Cubs regular. Knowing the career lengths of your turn-of-the-20th-century Cubs stars will bring you a two-bagger.

3 Just two years after winning their last pennant to date, the bottom fell out on the Cubs when they finished 6th in 1947 and stole an all-time club low 22 bases. The team co-leaders that year with a mere four thefts were Andy Pafko and what shortstop who finished his seven-year career with the Cubs that season by scoring just 24 runs in 108 games? Telling you that his grandson later caught for the White Sox should help you get off the mat and nail a double, plus a RBI if you also know the grandson's first name.

4 Which fleet second sacker one year swiped 54 bases for the Cubs in 61 attempts for a stunning .885 success rate but fell to 31 swipes in 45 tries the following season before moving elsewhere in the bigs? RBI single.

5 Before Juan Pierre was the runner-up in 2006, it had been well over half a century since a Cub has come so close to winning a loop stolen base crown. Who was the most recent previous Bruin even to tie for the NL theft-title runner-up spot? Two bases for him, and extra base for knowing the year.

6 Who is the only 40-year-old to pilfer as many as 40 sacks in a season? After years of productivity on the West Coast, he came to the Cubbies as a part-timer and continued his larcenous ways. In only 99 games one year, he snagged 47 bases in just 51 tries before moving elsewhere midway through the following season. Double.

7 In 1929, Cubs outfielder Kiki Cuyler swiped 43 bases. Fans waited over half a century for another Bruins gardener to filch as many as 40 bases in a season in the person of a man with 45 swipes for a Cubs club that won 96 games. For a few years he was the Bruins most wide-ranging center fielder since Pafko. Double.

8 A certain second sacker landed with the Cubs after establishing another franchise's career steals mark. During his lone season in Bruins flannels he topped the team with 35 thefts despite missing over 30 games. Few remember his given name was Elliott, but many recall his father, whose middle name was Morning. RBI double, plus an extra ribby for the club whose career theft record he currently holds.

9 Who is the only documented member of the Cubs to have been caught stealing as many as 100 times? We'll give you a big steer by noting that he made the Brazen Base Thief in the previous question expendable by assuming that performer's position. Single.

10 Ready to slap a gift double? In 1975 the Cubs stole just 67 bases as a team but more than half their total came from a speedy gardener who swiped 129 sacks during his six seasons in Wrigley.

AB: 10
Hits: 10
Total Bases: 20
RBI: 4

INNING 4
GOLD GLOVE GOLIATHS

1 Many have forgotten this moundsman's solid arm was also adept at nailing runners. His finest year with the leather was as a Cubbie when he became the only pitcher to record as many as 85 assists while fielding 1.000 in a season. Blocked from winning the Gold Glove first by Haddix, then Shantz, and finally Gibson, he's worth a double.

2 A strong case can be made that this man was the worst gardener the Cubs ever had based on his .826 career FA as a Chicago pastureman. But militating against that are his 206 assists, tied for the most ever by a Chicago outfielder. Easier than it looks, hence only a double.

3 When Billy Williams logged his 110th assist en route to his post-1901 Cubs gardeners' career record total of 143, whose old mark of 109 did he break? Apply an old kernel of wisdom here and con us out of a RBI triple.

4 Among all hurlers in as many as 200 games with the Cubs, whose name headed the list for the top career fielding average (.990) until the 1980s? Should help you to a RBI single learning that in his five full seasons with the Cubs he made only three errors, pitched on two pennant winners and won 98 games.

5 Among first sackers who spent as many as three full seasons with the Cubs, what slick-gloved lefty held the club season record with a .993 FA prior to Ernie Banks's move from short to the initial sack? RBI single.

6 Tinker, Evers and Chance played together more or less regularly for eight seasons from 1903 through 1910. Which two of the Cubs regular infielders during that span turned the most double plays of all NL players at their positions? Read that again carefully, but don't be caught thinking it's a trick question. You need both correct answers to score a triple.

7 In 1951 Randy Jackson accrued 323 assists to set a new Cubs season record for a third sacker. Whose old mark of 322 did he break? The only clue experts will need to homer is being told he has the most career at bats of anyone in major league history about whom it is still unknown which way he batted.

8 Two Cubs catchers with as many as 130 games behind the dish fielded .996 in a season. One copped a Gold Glove for his efforts and for a while proved to be one of the sturdiest backstops in the game. The other never recaptured his former glory and drifted to seven other teams before departing in 2001. Single for one, stretch it to a triple for both.

9 The first Cubs outfielder to win a pair of Gold Gloves actually captured eight total but the first six came with another outfit that now plays in a different city. Single.

10 Arriving in the Billy Williams swap, he paced NL second baseman in assists during each of his four seasons in the Windy City. Never a Gold Glover as a Cub, he would capture four straight with his next club. Double.

AB: 10
Hits: 10
Total Bases: 22
RBI: 4

INNING 5
HOME RUN KINGS

1 Who led the Cubs first division winner in round-trippers with 25 after sharing the club high in that category the previous year? Single for him and a RBI for the performer he tied that other season.

2 What former NL homer king topped the 1938 flag winners with a modest total of 13 taters? RBI double.

3 In 1884, playing in a fluky park with short fences, four Chicago performers hit over 20 homers. Name all four for a four-bagger. Single if you know just three.

4 Playing in a new park in 1885 with deeper fences, the Chicagos had just one man who homered in double figures, but his 11 homers were enough to give the Windy City crew their second straight NL homer leader. Who was he for a triple?

5 While many of the Cubs stars jumped to the Players League in 1890, Cap Anson remained loyal to the NL and so did a certain outfielder that came to the club that spring from the defunct Washington franchise. He rewarded his new team by topping the NL with 14 homers. Home run if you know him.

6 A part-time outfielder in his first three seasons with the Cubs, he blossomed in his fourth and led the club with 13 homers in 1915. The following year he led the NL with 12 homers and would later win three more HR crowns with another NL team. Many will breathe a sigh of relief if they notch this double.

7 In 1961, the final year prior to NL expansion, four Cubs topped 20 homers but only one member of the quartet also surpassed the .300 mark. His name will bring a RBI double.

8 What Cub holds the record for most homers in a season by a player who drew under 40 walks? Although he's remembered for his slugging stick, few realize that he never walked more than 44 times during his 21-year career. Single.

9 When Shane Andrews creamed 14 homers in 182 at bats in 2000, what backup backstopper's Cubs record of 13 did he break for the most homers in a season with less than 200 ABs? That 13 proved a truly unlucky number as our man clipped just five more homers and hit under .150 in his two remaining ML seasons, finishing with the 1993 Cardinals. Triple.

10 The youngest Cub to splat as many as 20 homers in a season was a mere 21 when he slammed 23. That was just the beginning as he smote as many as 20 on 11 occasions in all for the Bruins. Single.

AB: 10
Hits: 10
Total Bases: 23
RBI: 5

MASTER MOUNDSMEN

1 No Cubs hurler since 1900 has fanned 300 batters in a season. What Chicago NL hurler did it twice prior to 1901? RBI single.

2 What tosser holds a share of the modern Cubs season record for the most shutouts (9) as well as a share of the all-time ML season record with 16? Single.

3 Who are the only two hurlers among the top 10 in all-time ML wins that wore a Chicago NL uniform? You need both for a single.

4 Remarkably no pitchers among the top 10 all-time in losses ever labored for the Cubs. Who is the only one among the top 15 to wear Cubs livery? The lone clue you should need to double is that the final three of his 245 losses came with the Cubs.

5 Although known for his control, he is the Cubs all-time leader in most batters hit by pitches with 85. Tough triple.

6 This one may be more challenging than we think so we'll award a double. Who was the Cubs all-time leader in pitching strikeouts prior to NL expansion in 1962?

7 Who won the most career games among Cubs southpaws since World War II? He led the Cubbies with 84 victories in a certain decade despite being dealt three years before it ended. Double.

8 What two-time Cubs 20-game winner is the only Bruin to toss 300 innings in a season without yielding a homer? After he went 21-14 in 1903 in 312⅓ homer-free innings, club president Jim Hart accused this New Straightsville, Ohio, native of crookedness and shipped him to the Cards. RBI triple.

9 In 1946 this Cubs southpaw topped the NL in strikeouts and two years later went 18-13 with a 2.64 ERA for a Bruins team that lost 90. He was dubbed "Bear Tracks" due to his size 14 shoes, and you can try to fill them for a double.

10 Back ailments classified this Lunsford, Arkansas, righty 4-F in World War II, and he finished with a modest 79-70 career slate. However, he topped the wartime Cubs in wins for three straight seasons, with his final year of leadership coming on the Bruins last flag winner to date. Double.

AB: 10
Hits: 10
Total Bases: 19
RBI: 2

INNING 7
BULLPEN BLAZERS

1 Who was the first reliever to appear in as many as 250 games with the Cubs without ever saving as many as ten games in a season? Debuting as a starter in the AL, he joined the Cubs in 1979 and led the NL with 84 games from the pen a year later. Double.

2 Who converted a Cubs club record 26 consecutive saves over portions of two seasons? Before becoming the Bruins closer, he made a NL All-Star team as a starter, fanning over 200 batters by season's end. Fergie appeared in the most games among Canadian-born Cubs, but this man's second. Single.

3 In 1958 Don Elston set a new Cubs record when he made 69 relief outings. He still fell seven short, however, of the club's all-time season record at that time for pitching appearances. Who held it with 75? Double off the wall.

4 What former Red Sox starter set the Cubs pre-expansion record for the most innings pitched in a season, all in relief, when he logged $134\frac{1}{3}$ frames in 1959? Three-bagger.

5 What former member of the last Washington pennant winner to date became the first hurler in Cubs history to log as many as 100 innings in a season, all in relief, when he tossed $102\frac{1}{3}$ frames for the 1938 NL champs? Worth a double and two ribbies.

6 Who was the first Cubs lefty to work as many as 80 games in a season from the pen? This Springfield, Illinois, native logged 82 appearances and saved 12 games at age 38.

A true journeyman, he took the mound over 700 times with nine teams. RBI single.

7 Pitchers who carved out careers as relievers were scarce in the Deadball Era, but the 1918 NL champion Cubs had one of the best. Of his 127 career mound appearances, 84 came in relief, including 17 in 1918 when he tied for the club lead in saves with two and finished a team-high 10 games out of the pen. Three-run homer if you know the hurler whose nickname was a natural in his time given his last name.

8 He's well known to even modern-day Cubs enthusiasts for some of his early-day club batting exploits, but few know that he also holds the club's pre-1901 record for career saves, albeit with just three. His name's not Anson, but it was nearly as famous in its day. Two-bagger.

9 Who was the first blazer to fan 100 or more batters in a season, all in relief, wearing Cubs livery? Learning that his breakthrough year of 111 Ks came in the same season that a reliever was selected the World Series MVP for the first time should help you score a two-bagger, plus an extra two bases if you know the Series MVP.

10 Would it surprise you that the first Cubs pen blazer to average 11 strikeouts per nine innings in a season was neither their split-finger flinger nor that wicked 6' 5" Louisiana fastballer? Actually it was a flame-throwing setup man, who scorched 107 batters in just 82 innings for Don Baylor's crew. RBI single.

11 Who broke Bruce Sutter's club record for saves in a season? In just three years with the Cubbies this lefty blazer saved 112 and set a then–season NL record in this category. Bunt single.

12 Relievers who give up an average of more than one hit per inning are usually relegated to mopup roles, but the Cubs had a husky, mustachioed righty bullpenner one year who yielded 86 hits in a mere 80⅓ innings, yet not only led the league in appearances but compiled 51 saves, the most ever by a hurler who yielded more than one hit per inning. He went packing the following year and was never again used as a closer. Still, he compiled 260 career saves, all but three of them in the NL. A single for him and two RBI if you know whose record he shattered for the most saves by a reliever who surrendered more than one hit per inning.

AB: 12
Hits: 12
Total Bases: 25
RBI: 10

INNING 8
WHO'D THEY COME UP WITH?

Remember to credit yourself with two extra RBI for each debut year you know.

1 Monk Dubiel. Home run.

2 Claude Passeau. Triple

3 Jack Pfeister. Home run.

4 Lee Walls. Double.

5 Bill Hutchison. Two-run homer for the team alone and your name in lights in the trivia Hall of Fame if you also nail the year.

6 Walt Moryn. Routine single for '50s fans.

7 Ted Abernathy. Homer.

8 Sammy Sosa. Barely past the pitcher's glove for a single.

9 Ryne Sandberg. Another gift single.

10 Randy Hundley. Double.

11 Bill Buckner. Single.

12 Steve Stone. Triple.

AB: 12
Hits: 12
Total Bases: 30
RBI: 29

INNING 9
RBI RULERS

1 Who was the last Cub to collect 100 RBI in a season in which he fanned fewer than 30 times? Bat control was a forgotten hallmark of this four-decade infielder who quietly tallied more career RBI than any other player who whiffed fewer than 500 times since expansion. Though he'd be downgraded by *Moneyball* lovers who cringe at his failure to coax walks, we'll upgrade you to a double for his name.

2 The first Cubs second baseman to drive in 100 runs in consecutive seasons merits just a single.

3 Before Slammin' Sammy, who was the last Cub to hit .300 and drive in over 100 runs in the same season? A year later he collected less than 80 RBI but repeated as team leader. RBI single.

4 Which one of these men never led the Cubs in RBI? Frank Chance, Riggs Stephenson, Jerry Morales, Rick Monday or Dave Kingman. Single.

5 What Cub drove in over 140 runs one season but failed to lead the NL? That year he would have set the club season record in RBI had his teammate not topped the league. Double for both men and a RBI for the year.

6 Who led the flag-winning Cubs in RBI with 65 in the war-abbreviated 1918 season? Three-bagger.

7 Who occupied center field for the Cubs during most of their three-year reign as NL champs from 1906 through 1908 despite collecting just 91 aggregate RBI, the fewest ever by a regular on a team that won three consecutive flags? We'll also clue you that he debuted with Washington in 1899 by setting a new major league season record for outfield putouts. RBI double.

8 Gabby Hartnett holds almost every Cubs career fielding record for a catcher, but one he just missed is assists. Who topped Gab's career assists total of 1,239 with 1,244? Shouldn't be a difficult double if we throw in the fact that it was his club record for the most career RBI by a catcher that Gabby broke.

9 Who led the Cubs in RBI on the last flag winner managed by Frank Chance? Overshadowed by Tinker, Evers and Chance himself, he played on each of the Cubs first four 20th century pennant winners but saved his best for 1910 by plating 86 mates and topped the team with a .325 average. An unsung super-sub, he played every position but pitcher and catcher. Triple.

10 Who is the only Cubs Hall of Famer to collect 1,000 or more career RBI (not all of them as a Cub) without ever hitting 20 homers in a season? Three-bagger.

AB: 10
Hits: 10
Total Bases: 20
RBI: 3

GAME 6

INNING 1
HOME RUN KINGS

1 Who was the only Cub to slug as many as 30 homers in a season, yet fan fewer times than he went deep? Go for three.

2 Just four years after leading the AL in homers, he clubbed 25 dingers in his only season with the Cubbies. Shipped back to the junior circuit in a tumultuous trade, he was done by age 33. His name should ring your chimes for a double.

3 What former NL Triple Crown winner once led a flag-winning Cubs team in four-baggers despite being held by injuries to just 119 games? Single.

4 In 1926 he set a new Cubs record when he failed to homer in 624 at bats. The following year he broke his own mark by going homerless in 647 ABs, still the club record. Two-run triple.

5 In 1959 Ernie Banks clubbed 45 home runs, but he had little behind him. Even though the Cubs had seven other players post double-figure homer totals that year, none had more than 14. Name either of the pair whose 14 dingers tied for the runner-up spot to Banks in 1959 for a single; a three-bagger if you nail both.

6 The year following the first flag in Windy City history, the 1877 Chicago NL entry earned a negative power distinction that it is almost certain never to lose. Only true experts will know what it was and for it they earn a two-run dinger.

7 In his only full year with the Cubs, he became the oldest Bruin to swat as many as 30 homers in a season. Knowing that he reached that plateau with four other clubs makes it a crime for us to award more than a generous double.

8 A steady performer for 13 years in Wrigley, his 148 dingers are the most by any Cub who never clouted as many as 20 in a season. Possessor of a solid batting eye and a smooth glove, he closed with over 2,400 hits and a .303 average. You've got enough here to slap a single.

9 In 1928, Hack Wilson won his second straight home run crown. Two years later he won another title when he hit a then NL-record 56 dingers. What two Hall of Fame sluggers prevented Wilson from capturing four straight NL home run prizes by finishing ahead of his 39 dingers in the 1929 NL home run derby with totals of 43 and 42, respectively? You need both for a RBI single.

10 In 2006 Carlos Zambrano tied the Cubs post-1900 record for the most home runs by a pitcher with six. The hurler whose mark he tied also started the most career games of any twirler since 1900 that never tasted postseason play. Single for him and RBI for the year.

AB: 10
Hits: 10
Total Bases: 21
RBI: 6

MVP MARVELS

1 Either a league MVP Award or a Baseball Writers' Association of America Award has been given to a National League player every year since 1924 save one. What was the sole season in that span when no awards were given in either major league? Single, plus a RBI if you also know the Cub who would have been a heavy favorite to win it the year in question.

2 The youngest Cub to nab a MVP was 25 and hit 19 homers that year, less than half his personal best. Tally a RBI single for both him and the year but nothing for less.

3 What Cub was the first player other than a catcher, a pitcher or a shortstop to win a MVP Award with a sub-.300 batting average? Double, plus an extra base for the year he won.

4 What Cubs position player was runner-up for a MVP Award even though he played only 110 games and had less than 400 at bats? Three-bagger and a RBI if you also know the year.

5 Who was the only Cub other than Ernie Banks to earn as many as nine MVP votes in a season between 1953 and 1962? Home run.

6 The first Cubs pitcher in history to win the pitching Triple Crown—most wins and strikeouts and lowest ERA—did it in a year when no MVP prizes were given. However, he had the pleasure of cashing a World Series check. Name him and his magic season for a double.

7 What Cubs hurler won two legs of the Pitching Triple Crown—most wins and lowest ERA—the season he was runner-up to a Hall of Fame catcher for the NL MVP? Single for the pitcher and a RBI for the catcher who beat him out.

8 What more does a guy have to do? Despite leading the NL in hits, batting, doubles, slugging, extra base hits, total bases, OPS, and runs created, what Cubs star failed to cop a MVP? Just a single.

9 After Ernie's consecutive MVPs only one Cub from 1960–1971 managed to place among the top five vote getters twice. Name him for a single.

10 Who was the first Cub to earn MVP votes in a season he started with another team? Arriving that year in a late April swap, he notched a league-leading 25 saves with a 2.20 ERA. In parts of five seasons in Wrigley, he appeared in nearly 250 games before closing with the Pale Hose. Double, plus a RBI for the year.

11 At age 29, this Cubs outfielder missed winning the MVP by a single vote and never earned another MVP vote again. No one-year wonder, he finished third in the MVP balloting the year before and had notched a few in each of the three previous seasons. One of the most popular Cubs of his era, he clubbed over 200 dingers for the Windy City crew. Single.

AB: 11
Hits: 11
Total Bases: 18
RBI: 6

INNING 3
PEERLESS PILOTS

1 Who is the only man to date to debut with a major league team based elsewhere than Chicago in the state of Illinois and later manage a Chicago NL team? One base for the man and two RBI for the Illinois city in which he made his ML debut.

2 He played 14 years in the minors, earning the Texas League batting crown in 1957. Although this Ohioan never tasted big league java, he became the first manager ever to guide divisional champs in both leagues during his initial season at the helm of each club. Our clue that one of them was the Cubs downgrades this to a mere single.

3 Greg Maddux reached his zenith under the squinting stare of Atlanta's Bobby Cox. But what light-hitting short-stop and future Cubs GM served as the youthful hurler's first big league pilot? Double.

4 A certain shortstop hit just .203 in 212 career at bats with the White Sox and Cubs. Most Wrigley denizens have long forgotten his playing days but still remember him for serving as the Cubs skip during Sandberg's formative years on the club. RBI single.

5 Cap Anson is the Bruins career leader in RBI. Name the only other two men on the club's Top 10 career ribby list who also served as Cubs managers. Double for both and no credit for less.

6 What future pilot of a World Championship team cashed a winner's share Fall Classic check as a playing member of the last Cubs world champ to date? Triple.

7 The first Cub to swipe two NL base-stealing crowns, one undisputed and one shared, was also the initial man at his position to win two loop theft titles as well as the first man to debut as a catcher and later manage the Cubs. Work through these clues carefully to score a RBI single.

8 Do you know the lone man to pilot the Cubs to a pennant after making his ML debut under a team supervised by Connie Mack? The process of elimination alone should steer you to a triple.

9 Cap Anson was the first player-manager to hit as many as 20 homers in a season. How many times was Anson a league leader in four baggers while serving as Chicago's player-manager? All it takes to win a RBI single here is an educated guess.

10 Who piloted the first Chicago entry to capture a big league flag? Double.

AB: 10
Hits: 10
Total Bases: 17
RBI: 5

INNING 4
GOLD GLOVE GOLIATHS

1 Among Tinker, Evers and Chance, which was the first to play with the Cubs and which was last to wear a Cubs uniform as a player? Single for getting both right; no credit for just one.

2 Thirty-six years after his father hit .272 as a slick-fielding rookie shortstop with the Cubs, he claimed the Cubs shortstop job and proceeded to record the only unassisted triple play in Cubs history. The family name alone will get you a two-bagger.

3 Whose club record for the highest fielding average by a shortstop did Joe Tinker break when he earned a .940 glove mark in 1905? You'll need to know your club history to sail a two-run homer here.

4 Watch out for this offspeed pitch. Prior to Ernie Banks's arrival, Billy Jurges with a .975 mark in 1937 held the club record for the highest FA by a shortstop. Whose mark did Jurges break? Stretch out your gapper for a triple.

5 Who played the most games at short for the Cubbies? During his career he paced the NL at various times in fielding percentage, chances per game, assists, putouts and double plays. Later, he served as player-manager for their cross-town rivals. This two-time Gold Glover's a double.

6 What frequent All-Star bagged Gold Glove honors with the Cubs 12 years apart? Unlike the Cy Young or MVP Award, players rarely recapture this prize after being snubbed for so long. Telling you that his Cubs drought had nothing to do with his being snubbed drops this to an infield hit.

7 Since expansion, the Cubs have had several rifle-armed shortstops anchor the left side of their infield. Choose the one who holds the club season record for assists with 595 and stop at third.

8 What Cub earned five Gold Gloves by age 28 but none thereafter? Since he's the holder of the top eight spots in season assists by a Cub at his position, we're anteing up just one.

9 What Cub won nine straight Gold Gloves after serving regularly at another position during his initial season in the Windy City? Another bunt single.

10 From the team's inception in 1876 until the early 1920s, a dozen different Cubs catchers recorded as many as 100 assists in a season. However, the game has changed so greatly that only one Bruin backstop has reached the century mark in assists since then. He captured a Gold Glove that year and you'll snag a double for him.

AB: 10
Hits: 10
Total Bases: 20
RBI: 2

INNING 5
STELLAR STICKWIELDERS

1 Who is the lone switch hitter in Cubs history to collect as many as 200 hits in a season? Tough single.

2 Who holds the Cubs pre-1901 record for the most career triples by a catcher? The only clue you should need if you know your players is that he had 34 career triples but only 53 walks. Two-run triple.

3 No pitcher since the close of the 19th century has accrued as many as 200 career hits in Cubs garb. Who came the closest with 195? May be tougher than it looks, so it goes for a three-bagger.

4 Who is the only NL hurler since Al Spalding's day to compile a .300 or better career batting average with as many as 200 at bats while serving mainly as a pitcher in a Chicago uniform? Three-run homer.

5 High slugging averages and low batting averages are commonplace nowadays, but do you know who was the only Cubs stickman prior to NL expansion in 1962 with as many as 1,000 career at bats to compile a .430 or better slugging average in conjunction with a sub-.260 batting average? Two-run homer.

6 Gabby Hartnett collected 1,179 RBI, a major league record at the time for catchers. How many 100 RBI seasons did he enjoy? Okay, a double.

7 No switch-hitting batting title qualifier has hit .300 for the Cubs since before World War II. However, this third baseman came within a point of that figure (.299) when he cracked 163 hits in 546 at bats. Learning that he had the same first and last name as the 1994 AL ERA champ makes this one worth only a single.

8 Only one Cubs regular since the 1930s has hit better than .325 three times. Interestingly, he never stroked 200 hits or batted higher than .331. Grab a gift single for this model of consistency.

9 Who holds the Cubs career pinch-hit record? After this gardener's first five seasons, at age 29 he set the new team career standard with 50 before drifting to three other clubs. Never a batting title qualifier, he's best remembered for hitting over .320 as a freshman. RBI double.

10 Across 18 seasons, he played for nine clubs, but this outfielder's Cubs years were his most productive as he topped .300 twice and missed a third .300 season by one hit. Many Cubs cranks remember his showboating more than his stick, so we'll wager a single you can't recall him now.

AB: 10
Hits: 10
Total Bases: 22
RBI: 8

INNING 6
SHELL-SHOCKED
SLINGERS

1 What Cubs hurler logged a .600 winning percentage (15-10) despite surrendering a post-1900 record 155 earned runs and a dismal 6.20 ERA, the worst ever by a NL pitcher in 200 or more innings? Figure out the year this unlikely feat happened, and you're well on the way to beating your way out of the jungle of bad Cubs hurlers to nail our man for a double.

2 Rare is the 20-game winner who allows as many as 30 home runs. Rarer still is the 30-game winner who does so. In fact, there are only two in all of history, and each, oddly enough, surrendered exactly as many homers as he had wins. One was Denny McLain in 1968 and the other was a Chicago hurler who was clubbed for 35 round-trippers in a season a good bit earlier. Nail him for a RBI double.

3 Even though he notched a neat 2.06 ERA in 43⅔ innings with the Cubs in 1911, the Bruins didn't like what they saw and let him drift off to the Braves. Turned out the Cubs were right as he proceeded to rack up a composite 5.30 ERA with Chicago and Boston in 1911, the worst ever by an ERA qualifier during the Deadball Era (1901–19). Even knowing he bore a first name that is pronounced the same as that of a mainstay on the last Cubs World Series winner to date forces you to buck the odds to claim a home run.

4 Who became the first Cubs hurler to surrender as many as 20 homers in a season subsequent to the pitching distance being set at 60' 6" in 1893 when he was taken deep 21 times in 1924? Two-run homer.

5 He was a regular in the rotation on two Cubs flag winners but nonetheless set a negative post-1901 club record by an ERA qualifier in one of those seasons when he allowed 15.8 enemy bases runners per nine innings en route to logging a 10-9 record and a 5.42 ERA. Two-run two-bagger for this career 100-game winner from the town of Comanche.

6 After he began his career as a reliever, the Cubs moved him into the rotation where he rewarded them with a NL lead-tying 22 losses, followed by a then-record-knotting eight balks the next year. Although he improved to 13-15, he was actually less effective, hiking his ERA to 4.71. That season his crowning achievement came when he set a major league record by allowing hits to the first seven batters who faced him in one of his starting assignments. Hustle to a double.

7 Acquired for Shawn Boskie, this Evanston, Illinois, native developed a penchant for surrendering homers. Over parts of five seasons as a Cub, he yielded 83 seat-reachers in just 89 games, including one season when he was tagged for 32 in fewer than 170 innings. Single.

8 During his 11-game Cubs career in the 1960s, this Springfield, Illinois, native posted a 6.14 ERA. He failed to make it past the fourth inning in each of his last four starts with the Cubs and in his final inning of work yielded a grand slam to Willie Stargell. Oh, did we mention he's a Hall of Famer? RBI double.

9 En route to losing a league worst 18 games, he also logged the highest ERA of any Cubs qualifier in nearly 70 years. Interestingly, he also led the Bruins in cumulative victories during that decade but only once topped them in wins for a season. Double.

10 Since 1900, who is the only Cubs chucker with as many as 100 starts in Bruins garb to average as many as ten hits surrendered per nine innings? In his four-year stay in Wrigley he went 28-41 before moving to the White Sox in 1981. Converted to a reliever, he retired in 1992 with over 350 games out of the pen. Double.

AB: 10
Hits: 10
Total Bases: 23
RBI: 7

INNING 7
MASTER MOUNDSMEN

1 What 200-game winner is the only hurler to start as many as 30 games in a Cubs uniform for eight straight seasons? This one's not as easy as it might look so we'll offer a triple.

2 Only two Cubs have won as many as 24 games in a season since Charlie Root bagged 26 in 1927. Triple for both and a RBI for each year, nada for just one.

3 What tosser won 20 for a Cubs team that finished with a losing record and two years later bagged 19 when they closed 18 games under .500? In his last productive season, this Mississippi master won 17 for a Bruins pennant winner. Double.

4 During the decade of the 1990s only two Cubs ERA qualifiers posted figures below 3.00. Both feats occurred in the same season, as the pair combined for 36 of the Bruins 78 victories. Score a double for them and a RBI for the year.

5 What hurler set a Cubs post-1900 club record for the most wild pitches in a season with 26 in the process of logging his third straight 20-win season with the Bruins? Once informed that he set a new club wild-pitch record in each of his three consecutive 20-win seasons, you've got a firm bead on a four-bagger.

6 Name the glass-armed Hall of Famer who posted a dazzling .875 winning percentage to go with a 1.81 ERA for the most recent Cubs postseason crew to appear in Yankee Stadium. Double for him, RBI for the year.

7 Three years after he paced the NL in fewest baserunners allowed per nine innings, a certain Cubs righty set a still-existing club record when he was tagged for 38 homers. We'll tell you it wasn't Bob Rush or Fergie Jenkins and still award a RBI double.

8 Despite all the loveable losers that have paraded across Wrigley's mound, only one Cub since 1900 suffered as many as 20 losses in a season twice. No bum, he had another season in which he won 22 and posted the second best ERA in the circuit. Three bases for this Lusk, Wyoming, lefty.

9 When he was in the box, Chicago went 44-19 and seemed headed for a certain flag. On the days someone else got the ball, the Windy City club was just 38-34, resulting in a second-place finish behind Boston. What year and pitcher are we talking about? Double for him and one base for the year.

10 Who is the only man to compile 20-win seasons for both the Cubs and White Sox? RBI single.

AB: 10
Hits: 10
Total Bases: 25
RBI: 7

INNING 8
ODD COMBINATION
RECORD HOLDERS

Imagine if Sammy Sosa had set the Cubs season record for the fewest strikeouts by a player with 50 home runs in the same season he established a new team mark for home runs. The Cubbies in this inning set odd combination records nearly as extraordinary.

1 Since 1913 when strikeout totals were first kept for hitters in both major leagues on a permanent basis, only one member of the Cubs has collected as many as 110 RBI in a season while fanning fewer than 30 times. He's not in the Hall of Fame despite debuting as a middle infielder and finishing with a career batting average above .335 for his 14 seasons, including nine as a Cub. Even with all that info, we think the deck is still stacked against most of our readers collecting a RBI double by naming the Bruins post-1912 season record holder for the most RBI with fewer than 30 Ks.

2 In the same recent season that Mark Bellhorn set a new Cubs record for the most strikeouts by a switch hitter, he eclipsed another negative record that was previously held by Woody English with 59 RBI in 1930. RBI triple if you know what it is.

3 The Cubs record for the lowest winning percentage by an ERA qualifier with an ERA below 3.00 belongs to a hurler who amazingly led his league in winning percentage the previous year. After going 25-10 with a 2.20 ERA, he saw his winning percentage shrink to .250 when his ERA with the Cubs remained a highly respectable 2.57. We'll chip in that his loop-leading winning percentage the previous year did not come with a NL team and still mark you up for a two-run homer.

4 In 1896, Bill Dahlen registered a .553 slugging average, the highest season mark ever by a Chicago NL performer with less than 10 home runs. Who is the only Cubs bat title qualifier since 1896 to post a .500 SA with less than 10 dingers? Solo homer.

5 Hurlers who allow an average of more than 14 baserunners per nine innings generally have ERAs well over 5.00. In 1942 what rookie set an all-time Cubs record for the lowest ERA by a qualifier who put on more than 14 baserunners per game (14.32) when he came in at 3.68? Our noting that the following year he stunned everyone by leading the NL in shutouts should prickle your ears and help you nail a two-run double.

6 In 1998, Sammy Sosa creamed 66 homers, the most ever in a season by a Cub who failed to hit a triple. Almost all team records like Sosa's belong to post-expansion players. Prior to 1962, only one Cub hit as many as 20 home runs in a season without hitting a triple. It happened in 1957 when a lefty swinger slammed 21 tripleless taters and a second lefty-swinging Cub was close behind him with 19. The record prior to 1957 was eight, set in 1942 by utilityman Rip Russell. For a two-bagger, name both the slowpoke lefty hitters who shattered Russell's former club mark in 1957. Sac hit for knowing just one.

7 Who is the only Cubs performer to log 20 or more triples in a season while stroking less than 20 doubles? We'll note that he led the NL the season in question with 21 triples despite collecting just 15 doubles. After adding that he set the all-time Cubs record that year for triples by a player at his position and that he also led the team in homers with 14, we say you should streak to a triple of your own here, provided you know his position, too.

8 The Chicago NL crew one season had a pitcher that surrendered 123 walks while logging just 39 strikeouts. Not surprisingly he had a 5.84 ERA and won just five games. The following year, however, he bagged 21 victories for Chicago and in the process became the last pitcher in history to notch a 20-win season after debuting in a major league that did not permit its hurlers to throw overhand (the American Association in 1884). All by himself, this chucker is good for a swarm of odd record combinations, and you're good for a two-run triple if you snare him.

9 Since 1893 when the pitching distance was lengthened to 60' 6" only one Chicago NL hurler has enjoyed a season in which he hit .300 and logged as many as 25 RBI. It was by no means a fluke season. Although its owner is seldom mentioned on lists of the best-hitting pitchers, he tops all hurlers with as many as career 500 at bats in a Chicago NL suit in batting average and is second in RBI with 117. Need we mention that he also tops a lot of odd combination record pitching lists? Two-bagger.

10 Which player who led the Cubs in steals four times, snagging over 30 twice, also holds the Bruins record for most games played in a season without swiping a single sack? He performed too well at Wrigley for us to offer more than a double.

AB: 10
Hits: 10
Total Bases: 27
RBI: 7

INNING 9
RED-HOT ROOKIES

1 What rookie forced Heinie Zimmerman to wait a year before claiming the Cubs third base post when he slashed NL pitching to the tune of a .282 BA in 1910, only to die that winter of surgical complications? All-around sports fans will gobble up a homer when we add that his name's the same as the Cleveland-born boxer that was killed in the ring in a 1947 title fight with Sugar Ray Robinson at the Cleveland Arena.

2 Few remember the rookie that shared first base with Phil Cavarretta in 1949 and also played an occasional game in right field before mysteriously dropping from view after slapping a solid .280 in 106 games and leading all NL first sackers in assists. Hence we feel it's appropriate to award a solo homer here.

3 Who held the Cubs season record for strikeouts by a batter prior to Sosa? Look no further than this rookie outfielder who stroked 16 homers and edged Donn Clendenon by one to top the NL in whiffs. Never again a regular, he's worth a double.

4 After winning the Chicago centerfield job as a rookie in 1879, he won the NL batting title the following year when he rapped .360. Two-run double.

5 Despite setting the Cubs post-1900 mark for runs by a freshman, he placed a distant sixth in that year's Rookie of the Year balloting. Scoring became a habit as he crossed the plate over 1,300 times in a Cubs uniform. Single.

6 While everyone crowed about Tom Seaver's, Dick Hughes's and Gary Nolan's freshman sparkle, that same year this Cub quietly topped all rookie southpaws with 13 wins. Sadly, that was his zenith as he slipped to 7-12 before waving goodbye two years later. Double.

7 Willie Mays won the NL Rookie of the Year over this Cub who led all senior circuit frosh in games, at bats, hits, doubles, RBI, runs, and steals. We'll reward you handsomely for his name with a double, plus a RBI for the year.

8 His arrival toward the end of the 1931 season made the Cubs willing to part with Rogers Hornsby the following year, and he didn't disappoint, rapping 206 hits in his first full year as the Bruins long-time second baseman. Just a single.

9 As a Cubs frosh in 1991, he topped the club with 27 thefts in just 56 games, the most for anyone in a season during the 1990s who played fewer than 60 contests. Never again seen in Bruins garb, he reappeared two years later with the Mets but retired with fewer than 100 games to his credit. If you said his name, stop at third and take two RBI.

10 After being buried for years in the Brooklyn farm system, this 28-year-old catcher finally caught a break when the Dodgers let him slip away to the Cubs prior to the 1952 season. He proceeded to lead the senior loop in batting in the early weeks of the campaign and finished at .290 while playing 101 games behind the dish. Nonetheless, he missed out on being selected for the All-Star Game and later was snubbed in the Rookie of the Year balloting, failing to garner a single vote. All but fans who date back to the 1950s will do well to triple.

AB: 10
Hits: 10
Total Bases: 24
RBI: 6

GAME 7

INNING 1
STRIKEOUT KINGS

1 Who holds the Cubs record for strikeouts in a season by a lefty reliever? In 1991 he fanned 117 in just 102⅔ innings but never reached the century mark in Ks at any other point in his 15-year career. RBI single.

2 Three Chicago hurlers took their turns at leading the NL in strikeouts prior to the turn of the 20th century. Each of the three is worth a base, but no credit given for less than all of them.

3 Who held the Cubs post-1900 season K record prior to 1967? Romp to a three-bagger and an extra base if you know this rookie's super K season. We'll even tell you that he was the youngest Cub since 1900 to fan 200 until Kerry Wood came along.

4 The only Cubs lefty to fan as many as 200 batters in a season will buy only a single these days.

5 Who held the Cubs all-time season record for the most Ks by a southpaw prior to the club's move to Wrigley Field? Don't be a rube and miss out on a triple here.

6 You'll be big on your block if you score a two-bagger for knowing the Cubs southpaw season K record holder prior to 1970.

7 Who was the first Cub to average more than a strikeout per inning in a season workload of at least 150 innings? This one's a bit tougher than it looks, so score a RBI double.

8 Name the only hurler who registered as many as 200 Ks for a Cubs team that won as many as 100 games. RBI double.

9 Who, at age 22, sported the lowest season ERA since the Deadball Era for a Cubs hurler with as many as 200 Ks? Caught between two choices? Choose wisely for a single.

10 Since 1920, only one Chicago hurler has led the NL in strikeouts for two straight seasons. His totals were less than 200 in each year, and during his initial leadership season this righty dropped a major league leading 20 games. Take a double for him and a RBI for nailing both of his big K campaigns.

11 Besides whiff masters Kerry Wood and Mark Prior, only one other Cubs ERA qualifier has averaged more than a K per nine innings, and like the other two, he did it more than once. Not bad for a performer who spent just three seasons in Wrigley. RBI single.

> **AB:** 11
> **Hits:** 11
> **Total Bases:** 24
> **RBI:** 5

INNING 2
WHO'D THEY COME UP WITH?

Remember to take two RBI for each debut year you score.

1 Rick Sutcliffe. Single.

2 Three Finger Brown. Double.

3 Don Cardwell. Home run.

4 Orval Overall. Two-run Single.

5 Abner Dalrymple. Triple.

6 Chuck Klein. Bunt single.

7 Bill Hands. Double.

8 Leon Durham. Single.

9 Ivan DeJesus. Double.

10 Dick Tidrow. Double.

11 Bill Nicholson. Homer.

12 Dale Long. RBI double.

> **AB:** 12
> **Hits:** 12
> **Total Bases:** 25
> **RBI:** 29

INNING 3
STELLAR
STICKWIELDERS

1 Who was the first Cubs slammer in the 20th century to hit .350 or better? Think carefully and you've hustled yourself to an infield hit.

2 Many AL teams have hitters who can make this claim due to the DH rule, but the Cubs have had only one batting title qualifier who posted a season OPS over 1.000 without playing as many as 80 games at any one position. The reminder that it was his single in that year's All-Star Game that sent Pete Rose careening into Ray Fosse with the winning run shaves him to a single and a RBI for the year.

3 Heading into the 1962 NL expansion season, who held the record for the most career switch hits in Cubs garb? RBI single.

4 When Roy Smalley, Jr., cranked out 21 homers in 1950, whose ancient record for the most home runs by a Chicago NL shortstop did he break? Double, plus an RBI for the year.

5 What season produced three of the top 15 batting averages in Cubs history by bat title qualifiers? Need the year and the three stellar stickmen to score a three-bagger; no credit for anything less.

6 What Cub set a NL record (later broken) by slapping 114 doubles over a two-season span? In so doing, he also established the team best for hits in two consecutive campaigns with 438. Single.

7 Since 1920, who has legged out the most career three-baggers in a Cubs uniform? Finishing just one shy of 100, remarkably he clubbed more triples than homers. RBI single.

8 In his five-year Cubs stint, he belted over 100 homers, leading the team thrice in dingers, including a personal best of 32 before being dealt westward. A single comes your way for this former Arizona State standout.

9 Who holds the Cubs record for most times reaching base in a season? He split the season between two positions, short and third. Prior to his death in 1997, he could boast of being the last surviving selectee to the inaugural All-Star Game in 1933. RBI double.

10 After signing as a free agent with the Cubs, what much traveled infielder hit a team-leading .314 as their regular second baseman, only to miss over half the following season with an injury before inking another free agent deal elsewhere? Single.

AB: 10
Hits: 10
Total Bases: 15
RBI: 5

TEAM TEASERS

1 In a certain season Chicago set a 19th century NL record by winning 21 straight games, including one tie. What year was it and what rookie Cleveland second baseman who was later a batting title winner ended the streak with a game-winning ninth inning home run? Double for the season and three RBI for the second sacker.

2 Name the season the Cubs featured this infield: 1B Preston Ward and Phil Cavarretta; 2B Wayne Terwilliger; SS Roy Smalley, Jr.; 3B Bill Serena. Worth a double, plus an extra base for identifying which of the five had the most total bases that year.

3 The first Cubs team to feature four sluggers who clocked as many as 30 homers each won 89 games but still finished 16 games out of first in its division. A single for the year and a RBI for each member of the quartet.

4 Can you name the four regular position players on the 1929 flag team that were still regulars on the 1932 team? Triple for all four; single for three; zip for less than three, but a RBI if you also know which of the four was playing a different position in 1932.

5 What 20th century Cubs team tied the club record by winning 21 straight games? Single.

6 Just four years after Cap Anson's retirement, the Chicago NL team amazingly had only one remaining player who been a teammate of Anson's. Who was it and what two seasons are we talking about? Tough two-run homer even for those who really know their history; no credit for knowing only the years involved.

7 A grand slam and then some is yours to pull in if you know the only man to be a teammate of Cap Anson's on both the Chicago NL squad and another major league team. Remember that we consider the National Association to have been a major league.

8 The first Cubs entry to post a team ERA over five since the days of Anson actually repeated the trick the following year. In both seasons their ERA leader was a righty from Council Bluffs, Iowa, who won 20 for them a year later. A single for both seasons and a RBI for the chucker.

9 What was the most recent Cubs team to commit more errors than games played in a non-strike year? The club played less than .400 ball, posting its worst record since 1966. Double.

10 What Cubs squad was the first in NL history to draw 1,000,000 fans at home? They finished fourth that season but two years later won the flag. RBI double.

11 Excluding strike years, what was the first Cubs team without a pitcher who won as many as ten games? Two men shared the club lead with nine. One was their closer, and the other never won in double figures during his six Cubbie seasons but retired with 163 victories. Double for the year and a RBI for each chucker.

> **AB:** 11
> **Hits:** 11
> **Total Bases:** 26
> **RBI:** 20

INNING 5
TUMULTUOUS TRADES

All of these transactions played a major part in Cubs history.

1 Would you trade a 32-year-old fading starter who went 6-11 with a 4.57 ERA? Not sure? What if you knew he had tendonitis and battled the bottle? The Cubs unloaded just such a righty for three future nobodies and even had to pay part of his salary to persuade that club to take him. Need we mention that he resurrected his career so famously that Cooperstown called him on the first ballot? Double.

2 What future NL MVP did the Cubs squander for Phillies first sacker Don Hurst? True, his MVP year did not come in Philadelphia. But he posted an OPS over 1.000 in each of his last two seasons with the Phils and retired with over 230 career homers, whereas Hurst lasted just 51 games in Chitown and hit .199. Double.

3 Prior to the 1914 season, the Cubs and Braves swapped second basemen that had both hit .340+ in 1912. Alas, the Cubs got a man who would leave the majors after hitting just .218 in 1914 while the Braves snared a performer who would bag the NL MVP that year. You need both to triple; sac hit if you know only one.

4 The Cubs got Doug Clemens and two former 20-game winners for Lou Brock. For a double name the mound pair that won a grand total of seven games in Bruins garb. Need both to score here.

5 What player did Chicago acquire from Brooklyn in 1899 in exchange for long-time Windy City stalwart Bill Dahlen?

The new Chicago acquisition played under a shortened version of his last name and his days in the Windy City proved to be short as well. He lasted only 82 games with the 1899 Chicago crew whereas Dahlen was still in a ML uniform 12 years later. Two-run homer.

6 Whom did the Cubs acquire in exchange for Socks Seibold, Bruce Cunningham, Percy Jones, Lou Legett, Freddie Maguire and $200,000? Two-bagger, plus a RBI if you know the team the Cubs fiddled on this one.

7 What hill star did the Cubs snatch from the Phillies in May of 1939 in return for Joe Marty, Kirby Higbe and Ray Harrell? Two-bagger.

8 You can homer here if you know who came to the Cubs from the Reds in the same package with Hank Sauer in exchange for Harry Walker and Peanuts Lowrey.

9 Every Cubs fan knows his Bruins fleeced the Phils for Fergie. What two position players did Philadelphia foolishly include to sweeten the deal? Triple for both, single for one.

10 If you're looking for the best Bruins boondoggle involving a position player, this may be it. Who batted over .320 across eight seasons with the Cubs after arriving in exchange for Sparky Adams and Pete Scott? You'll get a well-deserved hazing if you didn't double here.

11 He was just 19 when the Cubs packaged him with Dick Selma to the Phils. Hence all but the first of his 200 career blasts came after leaving Chicago. He rates a double even after we throw in the clue that he finished his ML career with the 1985 White Sox, plus an extra base if you name the former All-Star outfielder the Cubbies received in the deal for him.

12 The Cubs dispatched Lindy McDaniel, Don Landrum and the immortal Jim Rittwage in return for two players who starred in the Windy City. Grab a double for both, but just a single for knowing only one of the two young prospects the Cubs siphoned from the Giants after the 1965 season.

AB: 12
Hits: 12
Total Bases: 31
RBI: 4

INNING 6
JACK OF ALL TRADES

What position did Gabby Hartnett play? Catcher of course. The players in this inning all played more than one position in their careers, and some played so many that they really had no primary positions.

1 Who played over 900 games at first for the Cubbies after serving as a regular outfielder for a NL flag winner? A severe ankle injury robbed his speed and necessitated a position switch at age 27. However, he continued to produce for years and didn't exit until after turning 40. Double.

2 Name the famous trio that played in the same Chicago infield with Cap Anson in the 1880s and was noted for each of its members being able to play second, third and short with almost equal dexterity. Need all for a double.

3 After displacing Ken Reitz as the Cubs regular third sacker, what performer never again saw action in a ML game at the hot corner after that season? Take a moment and you'll realize why we can't award more than an infield hit.

4 This stocky Texan raked in 106 RBI and hit .307 as a Cubs right fielder. Two years later he poled a personal best 27 homers as their regular at third. During his Bruins sojourn he also played a bit at first and could even be spied behind the dish. Double.

5 What turn-of-the-20th-century performer saw regular duty with the Bruins at second, third and short before jumping to the American League St. Louis Browns in 1902? RBI triple.

6 The only man thus far to be both a regular second base-man and a regular centerfielder with the Cubs led all NL gardeners with a .989 fielding average the lone year he saw full-time duty in the pasture. Two-run homer for the Cubbie who debuted at age 17 with Brooklyn.

7 What slugging southpaw first baseman caught portions of two games for the Cubs in 1958 and had been groomed earlier in his career by a wishful Branch Rickey to become a full-time backstop? Two-run single.

8 Signed by the Cubs for a reported $125,000 bonus in 1960, he became the youngest Cubbie since 1900 to debut at age 17 years and 9 months. His three-year Bruin stint con-sisted of just 49 games and a dismal .171 average. But in 1966, while with Evansville of the Southern League, he switched permanently to the mound and resurfaced three years later as a reliever with the White Sox. In 1970 he appeared in 51 AL games before exiting the show. RBI double.

9 What Cub clubbed 20 or more homers in four straight seasons while playing first base but earlier that same decade hit .312 with 22 homers one year tracking fly balls in Wrigley's pasture? Bull your way through this one and knock a RBI single.

10 Liking his power stick, the Cubs tried him at second, short, third and even stuck him in a few games at first. Despite slamming 23 homers and a like number of doubles in 1998, his notoriously putrid plate discipline made him a free-swinging, low OBP liability. Single.

AB: 10
Hits: 10
Total Bases: 19
RBI: 7

1 The Crab. Single.

2 Mr. Chips. Solo homer.

3 The Antelope. Triple.

4 The Mad Russian. RBI double.

5 Twig. RBI single.

6 Bub. Two-run homer.

7 The Mad Monk. Double.

8 Dirt. Two-run Double.

9 Wild Thing. Single.

10 Ryno. Check swing single.

11 Bear Tracks. Triple.

12 Husk. Single.

> **AB:** 12
> **Hits**: 12
> **Total Bases**: 25
> **RBI**: 6

INNING 8
HOME RUN KINGS

1 Who holds the Cubbies mark for homers in a season by a third baseman? Easy to misstep here, but we're still awarding just a single.

2 The first home run champ in history to bat right and throw left was a member of a Chicago NL club when he bagged his dinger crown. Fans who know their Cubs history say this is only worth a RBI double.

3 What Cub on July 26, 1942, became the first player in major league history to hammer three home runs in the first game of a doubleheader and then sit out the second game? You say you've never heard about this odd slugging feat? Perhaps you know him better for being the only man to play in the 1945 World Series despite not playing a single game in the majors during the regular 1945 season. Triple.

4 The only Cub to post three seasons in which he collected as many as 500 at bats but failed to homer spent over a decade in the Windy City. Never did he post an OPS that topped .700 but solid glovework was his trademark. If you've surmised he's a middle infielder, you're correct. But if you're thinking he played in Tinker's day, you better set your time machine way forward. Triple.

5 What slugger, who once led the NL in homers while wearing Cubs threads, holds the record for lowest career OBP among players who clocked as many as 300 career four-baggers? Double for him and a RBI for his Cubs leadership year.

6 Who snapped Sammy Sosa's 11-year reign as the Cubs team home run king? Single, plus a RBI for the year.

7 Who posted the lowest OBP among Cubs who cracked as many as 20 homers in a season? This slugger clubbed 21 dingers in 479 at bats and totaled just 28 walks for a puny .280 OBP. Snag a single for the man who shares the same first and last name with another clubber who starred in Pale Hose garb.

8 In 1950, for the first time since 1929, the Cubs had two 30-homer men. Name both for a two-run single. No credit for just one.

9 Who holds the Cubs record for four-baggers in a season by a switch hitter? In his only full season in Wrigley, this Billy Beane discard drove out 27 in 445 at bats. *Moneyball* devotees treasured how this infielder worked deep counts, but frequently it was more famine than feast for this scruffy free-swinger. Single for him and a RBI for the year.

10 Who held the Cubs rookie record for home runs until Ernie came along in 1954? An educated guess will buy little here, as he had only 15 career dingers, all in Cubs garb. Home run.

11 After Wildfire Schulte in 1911, the Cubs had to wait until the 1980s for another Cub to stroke 20 homers and swipe 20 bases. Name him for a RBI single.

AB: 11
Hits: 11
Total Bases: 20
RBI: 8

INNING 9
FALL CLASSICS

1 In 1907 what Cubs infielder led all regulars on both sides by hitting .471 against Detroit while slapping the Bruins only triple of the World Series? Step in and take three for yourself.

2 Who was the first Cub to blast a World Series homer in Wrigley Field? His shot off George Pipgras carried high into the rightfield bleachers, but we'll stop you at second for nailing him.

3 In 1932 who became the first Cub to power two homers in one Fall Classic? Four years later he became the last Bruins gardener to smack 200 hits until Billy Williams in 1964. Two-run double.

4 What Cub in 1910 became the first player to walk seven times in a five-game Fall Classic? Coaxing free passes came naturally as he topped the NL in both 1911 and 1912. Moreover, his totals those two seasons remain the highest ever posted by a Bruin, and in 1911 his free-pass figure established a NL record that lasted until 1969. Two bases.

5 It'll take a perfectly shot arrow to hit a bull's-eye triple by naming the Dublin-born backstopper who was the first man to play in a 20th century World Series for both an AL club (Detroit) and a NL club (the Cubs).

6 What Cubs hurler was removed after the first three batters singled against him in the final game of a World Series? Before booing him, bear in mind that he had previously started two games and relieved in another. Too, the Cubbies would likely have finished behind the dreaded Cards had they not acquired his services in late July from the Yankees. Single.

7 Sure the Yanks swept the Cubs in 1932, but you can't fault this Bruin's stick. In the opener, he became the first Cub to drive in three runs in a 20th century Series game. In fact, his eight hits in the four-game fray were more than any player on either side collected other than Lou Gehrig. Two bases.

8 Even though the Cubs lost the 1918 World Series to the Red Sox, they showcased the affair's top hitter. Sort through the club's batting order in your head until you're ready to choose the late-season addition who stroked a cool .389 against Red Sox hurlers that fall. RBI triple.

9 When the Cubs dropped the 1929 Series in five games, this refugee from the AL didn't help by hitting a measly .100 as their leadoff stick. In truth, our third sacker never played another big league contest after Game 5. Stop at third and watch two runners score ahead of you.

10 The only Cub to hit .250 or better in all three Fall Classics during the team's 1906–08 Series dynasty also was the club's leader in postseason hits during that span with 19. If we furnish the additional clue that his claim to being the team's all-time postseason hitting hero was only solidified by his showing in the 1910 World Series, everyone should burn his engine to race to a RBI single.

AB: 10
Hits: 10
Total Bases: 22
RBI: 6

ANSWER SECTION

GAME 1

Inning 1: RED-HOT ROOKIES

1. Bill Madlock, 1974–1976.
2. Larry Corcoran in 1880.
3. Eddie Stanky.
4. Bill Everitt.
5. Hack Miller.
6. King Cole in 1910.
7. Jerome Walton and Dwight Smith in 1989.
8. Gus Krock.
9. Scot Thompson, 1979.
10. Sam Jones, 1955.

Inning 2: HOME RUN KINGS

1. Bill Nicholson.
2. Jimmy Ryan.
3. Andre Thornton, with Cleveland.
4. Abner Dalrymple, 22 in 1884.
5. Tuffy Rhodes in 1994.
6. Vic Saier, who tagged Mathewson for five homers in his career.
7. Gabby Hartnett.
8. Alex Gonzalez in 1998
9. Sammy Sosa, whose 11 multi-homer games in 1998 topped Pittsburgh's Ralph Kiner (1949) by one.
10. Dale Long, Lee Walls, Bobby Thomson and Walt Moryn.

Inning 3: MASTER MOUNDSMEN

1. Nope, not Three Finger Brown—Fergie Jenkins, 1968–1971.
2. Johnny Klippstein.
3. Hank Borowy, 1945.
4. George Zettlein, 1874.

5. Knowing he was a moundsman rather than a boxman told experts that he pitched after the pitchers' box disappeared following the 1892 season and thereupon eliminated pitchers like Al Spalding, Jocko Flynn and Bill Hutchison, none of whom achieved both feats anyway—it was Nixey Callahan in 1897.

6. Fred Goldsmith, 1880.

7. Bob Rush.

8. Dick Ellsworth, 1963 with 2.11.

9. Charlie Root.

10. Ed Reulbach, .175 in 1906.

Inning 4: PEERLESS PILOTS

1. 1932, Rogers Hornsby and Charlie Grimm.

2. Tom Burns.

3. Frank Selee.

4. We'll give full credit for either 19 or 18½, as Anson took over early in the 1879 season and served through 1897.

5. Fred Mitchell.

6. Lou Boudreau.

7. Vedie Himsl, Harry Craft, El Tappe and Lou Klein.

8. Herman Franks, 1977–1979.

9. Whitey Lockman and Leo Durocher. Lockman replaced Durocher during the 1972 season.

10. Jim Riggleman, plus Joe McCarthy, Frank Selee and Jim Frey.

Inning 5: RBI RULERS

1. Andy Pafko.

2. Bill Dahlen, 1894.

3. Bill Nicholson, 1943.

4. Harry Steinfeldt, 1906.

5. Kiki Cuyler.

6. Ralph Kiner, led with 87 in 1953.

7. Just once, in 1990, with 100 and even then he had to share top honors with Andre Dawson.

8. Derrek Lee in 2005 drove in 107.

9. Wildfire Schulte.

10. Rogers Hornsby, 1931.

Inning 6: WHAT WAS THEIR REAL HANDLE?

1. Bobby.

2. Howard.

3. Mordecai.

4. James, known as Jimmy.

5. Emil.

6. Arnold.

7. James.

8. Elwood.

9. Bertram.

10. Kenneth.

11. Rufus.

12. Glen.

Inning 7: TEAM TEASERS

1. Poor you if you said the 1906 crew rather than the 1880 gang, which won at a .798 clip.

2. Ron Cey (97), Leon Durham (96), Jody Davis (94), Ryne Sandberg (84), Gary Matthews (82) and Keith Moreland (80).

3. The 1877 club, which finished fifth in a six-team National League.

4. 1925.

5. The 1909 bunch played .680 ball.

6. The 1945 team was 6-16 against St. Louis.

7. The 1962 Cubs lost 103 games, yet finished 18 games ahead of the woeful expansion New York Mets in the first season the NL schedule was expanded to 162 games.

8. 1969, Fergie Jenkins and Bill Hands.

9. The 2003 mound corps posted 1404 strikeouts.

10. In 1987, Andre Dawson led with 49.

11. Augie Galan CF, Billy Herman 2B, Frank Demaree RF, Gabby Hartnett C, Lon Warneke and Curt Davis were the pitchers.

12. In 1953, Phil Cavarretta served his final season at the Cubs helm, sneaking himself into 27 games and just 21 at bats.

Inning 8: ALL IN THE FAMILY

1. Randy and Todd Hundley.

2. Jim, 1909 Tigers.

3. Larry and Mike Corcoran.

4. Ray and Oscar Grimes.

5. Ad and Billy Gumbert.

6. Hal and George Jeffcoat.

7. Rick and Paul Reuschel.

8. Bobby and Barry Bonds.

9. Hal and Danny Breeden.

10. Gary Matthews, Jr. and Sr.

Inning 9: FALL CLASSICS

1. Will White.

2. Larry Corcoran.

3. West Side Park.

4. John Clarkson and Jim McCormick.

5. Bug Holliday.

6. John Clarkson and Mike "King" Kelly.

7. Abner Dalrymple, Milwaukee Cream Cities.

8. Fred Pfeffer, but nice try if you took the assist clue and guessed Ned Williamson.

9. Ed Reulbach in 1906, who also earned the Cubs first 20th century World Series victory that day.

10. Don Johnson, second base.

GAME 2

Inning 1: FAMOUS FEATS

1. Ernie Banks.

2. Ken Holtzman in 1967.

3. Ellis Burton.

4. Bill "Adonis" Terry and Ed Delahanty.

5. Dick Ellsworth.

6. Lon Warneke in 1934.

7. Babe Herman, in 1933; formerly starred for Brooklyn.

8. George "Zip" Zabel.

9. Sandy Martinez and Kerry Wood.

10. Frank DiPino, 1988.

Inning 2: HEROES AND GOATS

1. Steve Trachsel surrendered #62 after Mike Morgan gave up #61.

2. Jim Brewer.

3. Warren Gill.

4. The Great Chicago Fire.

5. Charlie Pick, the leading hitter in the Series.

6. Joe Tinker.

7. Joe Marty.

8. Don Hoak.

9. Phil Cavarretta in 1954

10. Sheriff Blake.

Inning 3: CY YOUNG SIZZLERS

1. Hank Borowy, 1945.

2. Jon Lieber, 2001.

3. Three Finger Brown, 1909.

4. Pat Malone, 1929.

5. Pete Alexander, 1920.

6. Clark Griffith.

7. Mike Bielecki, 1989.

8. Steve Stone.

9. Fergie Jenkins in 1971.

10. Ken Holtzman, actually he never earned a single vote his entire career.

Inning 4: BRAZEN BASE THIEVES

1. Ryne Sandberg who's fourth with 344.

2. Bill Lange in 1897.

3. Sparky Adams, 1925–1927.

4. Stan Hack, 16 in 1938 and 17 in 1939.

5. Richie Ashburn, 1960–1961.

6. Brian McRae.

7. Tony Taylor.

8. Adolfo Phillips.

9. Lou Brock.

10. Ivan DeJesus.

Inning 5: STELLAR STICKWIELDERS

1. No, not Ernie—Charlie Hollocher.

2. Lou "The Mad Russian" Novikoff.

3. Bob O'Farrell, .324 in 1922.

4. Bill Dahlen in 1895.

5. Billy Williams, 1629 singles edges Sandberg by five.

6. Cupid Childs.

7. Hack Wilson and Mark Grace.

8. Ivan DeJesus, shortstop.

9. Jimmy Sheckard.

10. Adolfo Phillips, 1967.

Inning 6: WHO'D THEY COME UP WITH?

1. Padres, 1997.
2. Troy, 1882.
3. Brooklyn, 1933.
4. Cincinnati, 1941.
5. Giants, 1923.
6. Pittsburgh, 1916.
7. Mets, 1989.
8. Padres, 1969.
9. Phillies, 1993.
10. Browns, 1923.
11. Orioles, 1957.
12. Dodgers, 1976.

Inning 7: MEMORABLE MONIKERS

1. Wildfire Schulte.
2. Bill Nicholson.
3. Dom Dallessandro.
4. Fred Pfeffer.
5. Bill Lange.
6. Charlie Grimm.
7. Gary Matthews.
8. Dave Kingman.
9. Ernie Banks.
10. Johnny Kling.
11. Don Zimmer.
12. Stan Hack.

Inning 8: FORGOTTEN UNFORGETTABLES

1. Don Young.
2. Sam Dungan.
3. Jake Weimer.
4. Hank Edwards.
5. John Sullivan.
6. Al Heist.
7. Randy Martz.
8. Jim Gleeson.
9. Dale Talbot.
10. Jim Davis, nephew of the Grissom brothers, Marv and Lee.

Inning 9: RBI RULERS

1. Fred Pfeffer, 101 in 1884.
2. Bob O'Farrell, 84 in 1923.
3. Ray Grimes.
4. Andy Pafko, 1948.
5. Jack Luby.
6. Cap Anson with 108 RBI.
7. Sammy Sosa in 2001.
8. George Altman, 1961 drove in 96.
9. Larry Doyle.
10. Frank Demaree, drove in 115 in 1937.

GAME 3

Inning 1: BULLPEN BLAZERS

1. Lee Smith, 625 Ks.
2. Paul Derringer.
3. Three Finger Brown, 1908–11.
4. Jesse Dobernic.
5. Turk Lown, 1957 and 1959.
6. Fred Beebe.
7. Charlie Root.
8. Bruce Sutter.
9. Ted Abernathy.
10. Mitch Williams.

Inning 2: HOME RUN KINGS

1. Oops—none other than Ralph Kiner.
2. Bill Nicholson.
3. Dave Kingman, 1979.
4. Joe Tinker.
5. Wildfire Schulte, 1910–11.
6. Sammy Sosa, 1993.
7. Johnny Moore.
8. Gabby Hartnett's 231 homers was passed by Banks in 1960.
8. Richie Ashburn, 1960.
10. Sammy Sosa.

Inning 3: MVP MARVELS

1. Ernie Banks, 1958–59.
2. Bob O'Farrell, 1926 Cardinals.

3. Wildfire Schulte, the first NL Chalmers Award selectee in 1911.

4. Rogers Hornsby.

5. Lon Warneke.

6. Phil Cavarretta, Hank Borowy and Hank Wyse.

7. Billy Williams, 1970 and 1972.

8. Sammy Sosa, 1998.

9. Andre Dawson, 1987.

10. Willie Hernandez, 1984 with Detroit.

11. Woody English.

12. Although Bruce Sutter placed seventh twice, it was Bill Madlock's sixth place tie with Steve Garvey in 1976.

Inning 4: NO-HIT NUGGETS

1. The Fred Toney–Hippo Vaughn double no-hitter on May 2, 1917, that was won by Cincinnati 1-0 with two hits in the 10th inning, including the game winner by Jim Thorpe.

2. Joe Borden with Philadelphia.

3. Larry Corcoran.

4. Chick Fraser.

5. Sam Jones.

6. Don Cardwell.

7. Bob Hendley.

8. Milt Pappas, in 1972, with Bruce Froemming the plate arbiter.

9. Burt Hooton in 1972.

10. Ken Holtzman in 1971.

Inning 5: WHAT WAS THEIR REAL HANDLE?

1. Cecil.

2. John.

3. Adrian.

4. Frank.

5. Charles.

6. Ransom.

7. Hazen.

8. Bryshear.

9. George.

10. Omar.

11. Nicholas.

12. John.

Inning 6: CIRCLING THE GLOBE

1. Matt Stairs.
2. Robin Jennings.
3. Heinz Becker.
4. Oscar Bielaski.
5. Hi Bithorn.
6. Tom Daly.
7. Fergie Jenkins.
8. South Korea.
9. Andre Rodgers.
10. Moe Drabowsky.

Inning 7: STELLAR STICKWIELDERS

1. Billy Williams, in 1964, 1965 and 1970.
2. Did you guess Ray Grimes? It's Dee Fondy, in 1952–1953.
3. Jim Canavan in 1892.
4. Zeb Terry.
5. Gary Gaetti.
6. Babe Twombley.
7. Not Hack Wilson; Rogers Hornsby with 409 in 1929.
8. Rick Wilkins, 1993.
9. Lee Walls, 1958.
10. Dave Clark.

Inning 8: RBI RULERS

1. Max Flack, traded for Cliff Heathcoat in 1922 between games of a doubleheader.
2. Frankie Baumholtz.
3. Fred Pfeffer.
4. Phil Cavarretta, 1945.
5. Vince Barton.
6. Roy Smalley, Jr., and Roy Smalley, III.
7. Andre Dawson, Montreal.
8. Sammy Sosa, 1995–2003.
9. Jody Davis, 94 RBI in 1984.
10. George Mitterwald.

Inning 9: RED-HOT ROOKIES

1. Ken Hubbs in 1962.
2. Jocko Flynn, 23 in 1886.
3. Charlie Hollocher, 1918.

4. Dick Drott, 1957.

5. Augie Galan.

6. Dutch McCall.

7. Les Lancaster.

8. Mel Hall, 1983.

9. Billy Cowan.

10. Eddie Waitkus.

GAME 4

Inning 1: HEROES AND GOATS

1. Gabby Hartnett.

2. Leon Durham.

3. Phil Cavarretta in 1945.

4. Stan Hack.

5. Three Finger Brown.

6. Larry French.

7. Bruce Sutter, 1978–79.

8. Max Flack misplayed the ball in the game started by Lefty Tyler.

9. Mark Grace, 1989.

10. Hugh Nicol.

Inning 2: FAMOUS FEATS

1. Cal McVey.

2. Pete Alexander, 72 Ks in 305 innings in 1923.

3. Ferguson Jenkins.

4. Randy Hundley, 1972.

5. None other than Cincinnati's Fred Toney, on May 2, 1917, in what used to be the one-of-a-kind "Double No-Hit Game."

6. John Hollison.

7. Bill Lee.

8. George Gore.

9. Jimmy Ryan.

10. Ernie Banks.

Inning 3: HOME RUN KINGS

1. Rogers Hornsby.

2. Henry Rodriguez.

3. Dave Robertson.

4. Earl Webb, and his record—ouch if you missed it—was the most doubles in a season.

5. Chuck Klein (40), Wally Berger (38), Babe Herman (35).
6. Hank Sauer, with 41 in 1954.
7. Glenallen Hill.
8. Rick Wilkins, 1993.
9. Jerry Martin.
10. Ryne Sandberg.

Inning 4: WHAT WAS THEIR REAL HANDLE?

1. Jesus.
2. Donald.
3. Jackson.
4. Harry.
5. Lewis.
6. Nathaniel.
7. Frank.
8. Myron.
9. Karl.
10. Steven.
11. Joseph.
12. Perce.

Inning 5: MASTER MOUNDSMEN

1. Ed Reulbach, 1906–08.
2. Pete Alexander, 0.89 in 1923.
3. Ned Garvin.
4. 2007 will be the 80th season since Bill Lee's 1938 winning-percentage crown.
5. Ray Prim, 2007 will be the 62nd season since his 1945 NL strikeout to walks ratio title.
6. Bill Hands, his 3.18 edges Fergie Jenkins's 3.20.
7. Guy Bush.
8. Hoyt Wilhelm.
9. Joe Niekro, 1968.
10. Clay Bryant and son Chuck.

Inning 6: MOMENTS TO REMEMBER

1. Shawon Dunston in 1982.
2. Claude Passeau, 1946.
3. Kevin Foster.
4. 1884, Ned Williamson and Cap Anson.
5. Hank Lieber.
6. Pete Scott.

7. Tony Kaufman.
8. Lou Stringer.
9. Cleo James.
10. Ed Reulbach.

Inning 7: PEERLESS PILOTS

1. Charlie Grimm, in 1932 second half, 1935, 1938 first half, and 1945.
2. Bob Scheffing, in 1958 and 1959.
3. Hank O'Day, 1914.
4. Frankie Frisch, 1949–1951.
5. Joe McCarthy, 1929.
6. Bill Killefer in 1925, plus Rabbit Maranville and George Gibson.
7. Jim Marshall.
8. Don Zimmer.
9. Leo Durocher.
10. Joe Altobelli, who guided the World Champion Baltimore Orioles in 1983.

Inning 8: RED-HOT ROOKIES

1. Billy Williams, 1961.
2. Bob Speake.
3. Ace Stewart.
4. Ed Reulbach.
5. Jack Taylor.
6. Bill Hutchison.
7. Jeremi Gonzalez, 1997.
8. Kerry Wood, 1998.
9. Burt Hooton.
10. Jack Curtis.

Inning 9: FALL CLASSICS

1. The Cubs hit just .195 while the Sox knocked a robust .198.
2. Orval Overall.
3. Jimmy Slagle.
4. Johnny Evers, 1910.
5. Kiki Cuyler.
6. Charlie Root.
7. Tony Lazzeri.
8. Carl Reynolds.

9. Mordecai Brown, 1906–1908.

10. Claude Passeau.

GAME 5

Inning 1: CY YOUNG SIZZLERS

1. Al Spalding, 1876.

2. Not Dick Ellsworth; it was Larry Jackson in 1964.

3. Milt Pappas, 1972.

4. Bill Hutchison, 1892.

5. Larry Cheney, 1912.

6. Rick Sutcliffe, 1984—and of course those lousy numbers were posted with Cleveland before he was traded to the Cubs.

7. Bruce Sutter, 1979.

8. Greg Maddux, 1992.

9. Rick Reuschel, 1977.

10. Carlos Zambrano, who earned votes in 2004 and again in 2006.

Inning 2: ALL IN THE FAMILY

1. Steve and Nick Swisher.

2. Hank and Ed Sauer.

3. Gene and Bill Lillard and Gene Bearden.

4. Jiggs and Tom Parrott, 1894.

5. Freddie and Chuck Lindstrom.

6. Don and Ernie Johnson.

7. Jack and Herman Doscher.

8. Mike and Greg Maddux.

9. Jim and Wayne Tyrone.

10. Chris and Justin Speier.

Inning 3: BRAZEN BASE THIEVES

1. Carl Reynolds.

2. Joe Tinker.

3. Lennie and Matt Merullo.

4. Eric Young, 2000.

5. Tony Taylor, 1959.

6. Davey Lopes, 1985.

7. Bob Dernier, 1984.

8. Bump Wills, Texas Rangers.

9. Ryne Sandberg, 107.

10. Jose Cardenal.

Inning 4: GOLD GLOVE GOLIATHS

1. Larry Jackson.
2. Mike "King" Kelly.
3. Max Flack, no relation to famed fictional con man Colonel Flack.
4. Lon Warneke.
5. Eddie Waitkus.
6. Johnny Evers led all second basemen with 362 and Harry Steinfeldt was tied with Art Devlin for the most by a third baseman with 118.
7. Barry McCormick.
8. Randy Hundley, in 1967, and Rick Wilkins, in 1993.
9. Andre Dawson, won it with the Cubs in 1987 and 1988 after starring with the Montreal Expos.
10. Manny Trillo.

Inning 5: HOME RUN KINGS

1. Ron Cey led in 1984 after tying Jody Davis in 1983.
2. Ripper Collins.
3. Ned Williamson (27), Fred Pfeffer (25), Abner Dalrymple (22) and Cap Anson (21).
4. Abner Dalrymple.
5. Walt Wilmot.
6. Cy Williams.
7. George Altman, .303.
8. Andre Dawson, 1987.
9. Hector Villanueva.
10. Ron Santo.

Inning 6: MASTER MOUNDSMEN

1. John Clarkson.
2. Pete Alexander, 1919.
3. Pete Alexander and Greg Maddux. Did you stumble here and say John Clarkson, whom Maddux recently knocked out of the Top 10?
4. Robin Roberts.
5. Ed Reulbach.
6. Charlie Root, 1,432.
7. Dick Ellsworth, 1960s.
8. Jack Taylor.

THE ULTIMATE CHICAGO CUBS BASEBALL CHALLENGE

9. Johnny Schmitz.

10. Hank Wyse.

Inning 7: BULLPEN BLAZERS

1. Dick Tidrow.

2. Ryan Dempster, 2005–2006.

3. Bill Hutchison, 1892.

4. Bill Henry.

5. Jack Russell.

6. Jeff Fassero, 2001.

7. Paul "Nick" Carter.

8. Ned Williamson.

9. Bill Henry and Larry Sherry, 1959.

10. Kyle Farnsworth in 2001 averaged 11.74.

11. Randy Myers, 53 saves in 1993.

12. Rod Beck, 1998; Randy Myers with 38 for the 1992 San Diego Padres.

Inning 8: WHO'D THEY COME UP WITH?

1. Yankees, 1944.

2. Pirates, 1935.

3. Pirates, 1903.

4. Pirates, 1952.

5. Kansas City of the Union Association, 1884.

6. Brooklyn, 1954.

7. Senators, 1955.

8. Texas, 1989.

9. Phillies, 1981.

10. Giants, 1964.

11. Dodgers, 1969.

12. Giants, 1971.

Inning 9: RBI RULERS

1. Bill Buckner, in 1982 drove in 105 runs and fanned 26 times.

2. Ryne Sandberg, 1990–1991.

3. Keith Moreland, .307 with 106 RBI in 1985.

4. Rick Monday.

5. Rogers Hornsby had 149 and Hack Wilson 159 in 1929.

6. Fred Merkle.

7. Jimmy Slagle.

8. Johnny Kling.

9. Solly Hofman.

10. Kiki Cuyler.

GAME 6

Inning 1: HOME RUN KINGS

1. Andy Pafko, in 1950 hit 36 homers and whiffed just 32 times.

2. George Bell.

3. Chuck Klein, 1935.

4. Sparky Adams.

5. Walt Moryn and Dale Long.

6. The 1877 entry was the last major league team to play a full season schedule without hitting a home run.

7. Fred McGriff.

8. Mark Grace.

9. Chuck Klein and Mel Ott.

10. Fergie Jenkins, 1971.

Inning 2: MVP MARVELS

1. 1930, Hack Wilson.

2. Ryne Sandberg, 1984.

3. Hank Sauer, 1952.

4. No, nobody in one of the strike seasons; it was Gabby Hartnett in 1937.

5. George Altman got exactly nine votes in 1961.

6. Hippo Vaughn, 1918.

7. Bill Lee and Ernie Lombardi, 1938.

8. Derrek Lee, 2005.

9. Ron Santo, who finished fourth in 1967 and fifth in 1969.

10. Phil Regan, in 1968 after coming from the Los Angeles Dodgers.

11. Bill Nicholson.

Inning 3: PEERLESS PILOTS

1. Cap Anson, Rockford 1871.

2. Jim Frey, won divisional flags with the Kansas City Royals in 1980 and the Cubs in 1984.

3. Gene Michael.

4. Lee Elia.

5. Gabby Hartnett and Phil Cavarretta.

6. Pat Moran, 1919 Reds.

7. After debuting as a catcher, first baseman Frank Chance shared the theft crown in 1903 and won outright in 1906.

8. Charlie Grimm.

9. Zero.

10. Al Spalding in 1876.

Inning 4: GOLD GLOVE GOLIATHS

1. Chance was first in 1898 and Tinker was last in 1916.

2. Jimmy Cooney and son Jimmy.

3. Jimmy Cooney, .936 in 1890.

4. Jimmy Cooney, son of the earlier-day Jimmy Cooney, .972 in 1926.

5. Don Kessinger, 1,618 games at short.

6. Greg Maddux, who won it in 1992 and again in 2004 after his lengthy stay in Atlanta.

7. Ivan DeJesus, 1977.

8. Ron Santo.

9. Ryne Sandberg, 1983–1991.

10. Jody Davis, 1986.

Inning 5: STELLAR STICKWIELDERS

1. Augie Galan, 203 in 1935.

2. Silver Flint.

3. Charlie Root.

4. Walter Thornton, .303.

5. Bill Serena, .251 and .439.

6. Just one, 122 in 1930.

7. Steve Ontiveros.

8. Mark Grace.

9. Dwight Smith.

10. Jose Cardenal.

Inning 6: SHELL-SHOCKED SLINGERS

1. Guy Bush, 1930.

2. Larry Corcoran, 1884.

3. Orville "Orlie" Weaver.

4. Tony Kaufman.

5. Tex Carleton in 1938.

6. Bill Bonham.

7. Kevin Foster.

8. Robin Roberts in 1966.
9. Steve Trachsel, with a 5.56 ERA in 1999.
10. Dennis Lamp.

Inning 7: MASTER MOUNDSMEN

1. Rick Reuschel, 1973–1980.
2. Larry Jackson, 1964 and Fergie Jenkins, 1971.
3. Claude Passeau.
4. Greg Maddux (2.18) and Mike Morgan (2.55), 1992
5. Larry Cheney in 1914.
6. Dizzy Dean, 1938.
7. Warren Hacker, 1955.
8. Dick Ellsworth dropped 20 in 1962 and 22 in 1966.
9. Bill Hutchison, 1891.
10. Clark Griffith.

Inning 8: ODD COMBINATION RECORD HOLDERS

1. Riggs Stephenson, 110 RBI with just 21 strikeouts in 1929.
2. Bellhorn notched just 56 RBI, the fewest ever by a Cubs batting title qualifier with a .500 or better slugging average.
3. George McConnell, 4-16 in 1916.
4. Phil Cavarretta, exactly .500 in 1945.
5. Hi Bithorn.
6. Dale Long, 21, and Walt Moryn, 19.
7. Vic Saier, 1913, at first base.
8. Bill "Adonis" Terry.
9. Clark Griffith.
10. Sammy Sosa, who failed to steal a base in 160 games in 2001.

Inning 9: RED-HOT ROOKIES

1. Jimmy Doyle.
2. Herman Reich.
3. Byron Browne fanned 143 times in 1966.
4. George Gore.
5. Ryne Sandberg, 1982.
6. Rich Nye, 1967.
7. Randy Jackson, 1951.
8. Billy Herman.
9. Ced Landrum.
10. Toby Atwell.

GAME 7

Inning 1: STRIKEOUT KINGS

1. Paul Assenmacher.

2. Larry Corcoran in 1880, John Clarkson in 1885 and 1887, and Bill Hutchison in 1892.

3. Tom Hughes, 225 in 1901.

4. Ken Holtzman, 202 in 1970.

5. Jake Weimer, 177 in 1904, breaking Rube Waddell's former club record of 168.

6. Hippo Vaughn, 195 in 1917.

7. Rick Sutcliffe, in 1984 fanned 155 in 150⅓ innings.

8. Orval Overall, 205 in 1909.

9. Not Kerry; it's Mark Prior, 2.43 ERA, 245 Ks, 2003.

10. Sam Jones, 1955 and 1956.

11. Matt Clement in 2002 and 2004; Rick Sutcliffe failed to be an ERA qualifier in 1984.

Inning 2: WHO'D THEY COME UP WITH?

1. Dodgers, 1976.

2. St. Louis Cardinals, 1903.

3. Phillies, 1957.

4. Cincinnati, 1905.

5. Milwaukee, 1878.

6. Phils, 1928.

7. Giants, 1965.

8. Cardinals, 1980.

9. Dodgers, 1974.

10. Indians, 1972.

11. Philadelphia A's, 1936.

12. Pittsburgh, 1951.

Inning 3: STELLAR STICKWIELDERS

1. Heinie Zimmerman, .372 in 1912.

2. Jim Hickman, 1970.

3. Augie Galan, 912.

4. Too bad if you took that ancient clue and ran to guess Ned Williamson. It was Bill Dahlen with 15 in 1894.

5. 1929, Rogers Hornsby (.380), Riggs Stephenson (.362) and Kiki Cuyler (.360).

6. Billy Herman, 1935–1936. The Cards Joe Medwick bested his two-year, two-bagger mark a year later.

7. Phil Cavarretta.

8. Rick Monday.

9. Woody English reached base 320 times in 1930.

10. Mark Grudzielanek, 2003.

Inning 4: TEAM TEASERS

1. 1880 and Fred Dunlap, 1884 Union Association batting champ.

2. 1950, Smalley.

3. 2004, Moises Alou (39), Aramis Ramirez (36), Sammy Sosa (35) and Derrek Lee (32).

4. Charlie Grimm, Woody English, Kiki Cuyler and Riggs Stephenson (ouch if you said Gabby Hartnett, who was injured for almost the entire 1929 season); English played short in 1929 and third in 1932.

5. The 1935 flag winner.

6. 1897 and 1901, Barry McCormick.

7. Bob "The Magnet" Addy, 1871 Rockford and 1876 Chicago; Cherokee Fisher and Denny Mack both played with Anson on the 1871 Rockford team and a later Philadelphia Athletics crew.

8. 1999 and 2000, Jon Lieber.

9. The 1980 club made 174 miscues in 162 games.

10. The 1927 outfit went 85-68, 8½ games behind the pack.

11. 1986, Scott Sanderson and Lee Smith.

Inning 5: TUMULTUOUS TRADES

1. Dennis Eckersley, traded to the A's in 1987.

2. Dolph Camilli.

3. Bill Sweeney and Johnny Evers.

4. Ernie Broglio and Bobby Shantz.

5. Gene DeMontreville (aka Demont).

6. Rogers Hornsby was robbed from the Boston Braves in the winter of 1928.

7. Claude Passeau.

8. Frankie Baumholtz in 1949.

9. Adolfo Phillips and John Herrnstein in 1966.

10. Hazen "Kiki" Cuyler, stripped from the Pittsburgh Pirates in November 1927.

11. Oscar Gamble was jettisoned during the 1969 offseason while Johnny Callison came from the Phils.

12. Randy Hundley and Bill Hands.

Inning 6: JACK OF ALL TRADES

1. Bill Buckner.
2. Ned Williamson, Tom Burns and Fred Pfeffer.
3. Ryne Sandberg.
4. Keith Moreland.
5. Barry McCormick.
6. Eddie Miksis.
7. Dale Long.
8. Danny Murphy.
9. Leon Durham.
10. Jose Hernandez.

Inning 7: MEMORABLE MONIKERS

1. Johnny Evers.
2. Bob Chipman.
3. Emil Verban.
4. Lou Novikoff.
5. Wayne Terwilliger.
6. Bub McAtee.
7. Russ Meyer.
8. Dick Tidrow.
9. Mitch Williams.
10. Ryne Sandberg.
11. Johnny Schmitz.
12. Frank Chance.

Inning 8: HOME RUN KINGS

1. Aramis Ramirez, 38 in 2006.
2. Jimmy Ryan blasted 16 homers in 1888.
3. Clyde McCullough.
4. Don Kessinger.
5. Dave Kingman led in 1979, and finished with 442 homers and an embarrassing OBP of .302.
6. Moises Alou, when he whacked 39 to Sammy's 35 in 2004.
7. Frank Thomas, 1960.
8. Andy Pafko (36) and Hank Sauer (32).
9. Mark Bellhorn, 2002.

10. Mandy Brooks, 14 in 1925.
11. Leon Durham, 1982.

Inning 9: FALL CLASSICS
1. Harry Steinfeldt.
2. Kiki Cuyler in Game 3 of the 1932 clash.
3. Frank Demaree.
4. Jimmy Sheckard.
5. Jimmy Archer.
6. Hank Borowy.
7. Riggs Stephenson.
8. Charlie Pick.
9. Norm McMillan.
10. Wildfire Schulte.

YOUR SCORE

Okay, now add up all your scores and find out where you stand. Be aware that the gentleman whom we regard as the greatest living Cubs expert batted well over .800.

AB:
H:
Total Bases:
RBI:

BA:
SA:

ABOUT THE AUTHORS

David Nemec is one of the best-selling baseball writers in the United States. His *Great Baseball Feats, Facts and Firsts* has sold over 700,000 copies in various editions, the most recent of which was coauthored with **Scott Flatow**. Between them, Nemec and Flatow have won ten National Trivia Contests sponsored by the Society for American Baseball Research.